Library of
Davidson College

DISCORDIA CONCORS

Kennikat Press
National University Publications
Literary Criticism Series

General Editor
John E. Becker
Fairleigh Dickinson University

Melissa C. Wanamaker

Discordia Concors

THE WIT OF METAPHYSICAL POETRY

National University Publications
KENNIKAT PRESS • 1975
Port Washington, N.Y. • London

Copyright © 1975 by Kennikat Press Corp. All rights reserved. No part of this publication may be reproduced, stored in a retrieval system, or transmitted, in any form or by any means, electronic, mechanical, photocopying, recording, or otherwise, without the prior written permission of the publisher.

Manufactured in the United States of America

Published by
Kennikat Press Corp.
Port Washington, N.Y. / London

Library of Congress Cataloging in Publication Data

Wanamaker, Melissa C
   Discordia concors.

   (National university publications: literary criticism series)
   Bibliography: p.
   Includes index.
   1. English poetry—Early modern, 1500–1700—History and criticism. I. Title.
PR545.M4W33   821'.4'09   75-15621
ISBN 0-8046-9089-8

IN MEMORY OF MY FATHER

CONTENTS

	Preface	ix
1.	THE HISTORICAL TRADITION	3
2.	JOHN DONNE: Yoking of Opposites	14
3.	GEORGE HERBERT: Discovery of Occult Resemblances	37
4.	HENRY VAUGHAN: Paradoxes of Regeneration	55
5.	ANDREW MARVELL: Unity in Multiplicity	71
6.	JOHN MILTON: Opposites and Multiplicity Resolved	98
7.	THE DECLINE	125
	Notes	137
	Works Cited	151

I especially wish to thank Professor Ernest J. Lovell, Executive Editor of *Texas Studies in Literature and Language,* for his kind permission to reprint in slightly different form my essay, *"Discordia Concors:* The Metaphysical Wit of *Silex Scintillans," TSLL,* 16 (1974): 463–77, © the University of Texas Press.

PREFACE

The suggestions, criticism, and encouragement that I have received from my former teachers at Columbia University, Professors Edward W. Tayler and P. Jeffrey Ford, have been invaluable. Professors Edward S. Le Comte of the State University of New York at Albany and Gwynne B. Evans of Harvard University have also read the manuscript at different stages and have generously offered much helpful advice. My mother deserves special thanks for the patience and kindness with which she has read, reread, criticized, and typed, large portions of this study. Mr. John Parke thoughtfully, and with care, styled the manuscript for the Kennikat Press. In various ways, each has made this book better than it might have been; the weaknesses that remain are, of course, mine.

The frontispiece from Hermann Hugo's emblem book, *Pia desideria*, is reproduced through the courtesy of the British Museum.

My appreciation of the British Museum staff and its superb facilities is especially deep. Butler Library of Columbia University also has my gratitude.

Original spellings are maintained in all quotations, except in the case of *i* and *j*, *u* and *v*, and the long *s*. To be consistent with this practice, I have modernized these letters in such contemporary editions as Frank Manley's text of Donne's

Preface

Anniversaries. For greater ease in reading I have expanded most contractions, omitted initial and terminal ellipses, lower-cased initial capitals in fragmentary quotations, upper-cased letters when they were set off by a colon or similar device. Long sections of italics in prose quotations are printed in roman when no special purpose seems intended.

DISCORDIA CONCORS

The seated figure may be likened to the metaphysical poet who, in his religious verse, attempts to transcend earth and grasp heaven through *discordia concors*, a yoking of opposites. From Hugo, *Pia Desideria*

ONE

THE HISTORICAL TRADITION

"Wit," like so many words fashionable three or four hundred years ago, is still current today; but between the seventeenth and eighteenth centuries its connotation changed radically. By the early 1600s "wit," derived from the Anglo-Saxon *witan*, meaning "to know," encompassed a man's entire mental powers, his imagination as well as his intellect; fancy combined with judgment to forge with great verbal dexterity new relationships that startled men of lesser mind.[1] But once that sense of harmonious unity and correspondence symbolized in the Circle of Perfection began to wane,[2] and once too that constellation of shared symbols—the dew, the circle, the microcosm and macrocosm, which represented these analogical correspondences—collapsed entirely before the end of the eighteenth century, it was no longer possible to regard wit as comprehending both judgment and fancy.

When Congreve and Farquhar were delighting Restoration theater audiences of the late 1600s and early 1700s with hilariously satirical comedies, wit had already become virtually divorced from judgment.[3] It consequently became mere wittiness, a comic art increasingly linked with fancy—the sparkle of clever repartee and playful flights of whimsy—connotations still associated with it. But to appreciate wit in its older, comprehensive sense as used by the metaphysical poets,

3

we ought not to expect the laughter that a *Beaux' Stratagem* arouses, and yet we may expect a kind of play in metaphysical wit. Perhaps nowhere is the play on words so pervasive, nor its aim so ultimately serious: to mirror wit, the mind of man, in all its shades and complexions, its colors and its complexities.

A further and even more important difficulty has long hindered an understanding of metaphysical poetry. There is virtually no seventeenth-century literary criticism—with the possible exceptions of treatises by Baltasar Gracián and Emmanuele Tesauro—that comments directly on the nature of metaphysical wit. Contemporary scholars have attempted to describe the phenomenon by various means, such as that of the baroque, the emblem and *imprese* (pictorial symbols), the far-fetched analogy or conceit, the meditation, and the "poetic of correspondence."[4] Although these explanations have furthered our understanding of the period, they tend to be imprecise (the baroque) or to explain only part of the phenomenon (the far-fetched comparison). Under the circumstances it seems obvious that we need a concept of poetry grounded in the period itself, one that is broad enough to encompass writers as diverse as John Donne and Henry Vaughan but precise enough to be useful in analyzing particular conceits and related lyrics. These requirements are met by *discordia concors*.

Discordia concors is a concept that provides an unusually direct approach to metaphysical wit. Since the combination *discordia concors* itself is an oxymoron, the rhetorical figure that joins contraries, the idea is readily associated with certain stylistic techniques, such as paradox, pun, and contraries. But even more significantly, *discordia concors* represents a particular world-view and particular relationships between a poet's beliefs and his literary style that may be successfully characterized within the confines of the seventeenth century.

When Dr. Johnson came to define metaphysical wit, he alluded to a philosophical tradition on which the writers of the seventeenth century relied but which has largely escaped the attention of modern critics:[5]

The Historical Tradition

Wit, abstracted from its effects upon the hearer, may be more rigorously and philosophically considered as a kind of *discordia concors*; a combination of dissimilar images, or discovery of occult resemblances in things apparently unlike. Of wit, thus defined, they have more than enough. The most heterogeneous ideas are yoked by violence together; nature and art are ransacked for illustrations, comparisons, and allusions.

The idea of *discordia concors* explains much about the metaphysical wit of poets such as John Donne, George Herbert, Henry Vaughan, Andrew Marvell, and John Milton. Since Earl Wasserman has already demonstrated the relevance of the concept to Denham's "Cooper's Hill" and Pope's "Windsor Forest,"[6] it is clearly time to reexamine earlier writers in similar fashion; for their wit, even more than that of Denham, needs to be "rigorously and philosophically considered as a kind of *discordia concors*." To my knowledge, this is the first book-length study that makes such an attempt.

Since Dr. Johnson's statements suggest that the philosophical concept of *discordia concors* is the basis for a literary style, the concept affords a justification for the metaphysical wit that Hobbes later considered "no better then Riddles."[7] Moreover, there emerges from Dr. Johnson's commentary a convenient though finally oversimple distinction between two major kinds of *discordia concors*, kinds that at least for the purposes of analysis may be seen as a broad spectrum ranging from mild dissimilarity to violent contradiction. The first pattern may be called "unity in multiplicity," an overarching harmonious blending of dissimilars. The second is a violent yoking of two opposites that logically contradict each other, a technique more characteristic of the astringent metaphysical style of the early 1600s than of the style of the poets scrutinized by Wasserman. The degree of discord between the terms united into a *discordia concors* may be compared to the dissentaneous arguments of Renaissance logic. In Milton's *Art of Logic*,[8] for example, "dissentaneous arguments" assert differences according to the intensity of opposition between terms. The two extremes of the spectrum—"diverse arguments" in which the terms are simply unlike (chair and chaise longue) and "contradictory arguments" in which the terms are violently opposed (hot and cold, dry and wet)—correspond exactly to the two kinds of *discordia concors*. If the terms of the *discordia concors* are diverses, the degree of dissentany that exists between them is slight, and the *concors* may be considered a harmonious unity in multiplicity. But if the terms in an argument happen to involve extreme oppositions like hot and cold or dry and wet, then the degree of dissentany approaches polar contradiction; and if the terms of the *discordia* are of this variety, we have Dr. Johnson's "yoked by violence together."

The pattern of *discordia concors* as unity in multiplicity served as an appropriate model for universal order in the Middle Ages, when the discovery of "occult resemblances" between diverse realms of existence was a customary and almost routine procedure.[9] But in the seventeenth century heaven itself seemed to recede from easy view and colloquy, and those gentler resolutions of discord no longer satisfied. "Where is my God?" cries George Herbert, "What hidden place/Conceals thee still?"[10] Accordingly, in their religious verse the metaphysical writers tended to leap beyond despair to yoke heaven and earth "by violence together," a *discordia concors* of opposites.

The two major branches of *discordia concors*, unity in multiplicity and the yoking of opposites, were both present in the early cosmologies of ancient Greece. Although the locution *discordia concors* (or its inversion, *concordia discors*) is of course Latin, the idea of *discordia concors* as unity in multiplicity begins in Greece as part of man's metaphysical quest to discover unity beneath the apparent vicissitudes of daily phenomena. In the philosophical system of Heraclitus, *discordia concors* is overtly equated with the doctrine of oneness in multiplicity.[11]

The bones connected by joints are at once a unitary whole and not a unitary whole. To be in agreement is to differ; the concordant is the discordant. From out of all the many particulars comes oneness, and out of oneness come all the many particulars.

And although Empedocles grounded his cosmology upon two fundamental and universal opposites, Love and Hate (or,

Concord and Discord), it is Love alone that in the best of possible worlds brings peaceful order out of warring chaos by unity in multiplicity. The single most important step in the development of the concept as unity in multiplicity was the discovery by Pythagoras that musical harmony has a basis in numerical ratios, which prepares the way for his other great principle—that the essence of the entire universe itself is number.[12] If everything is number, everything—even the most discordant and extreme—can be brought into a harmonious relationship (in Greek, "harmony" means "to fit together"). The universe of the *Timaeus*, for instance, is ordered upon a Pythagorean sequence of numbers; harmony reigns throughout creation—from the lesser, microcosmic human soul to the correspondingly greater, world soul, and finally to the Creator himself, in whose pattern all has been drawn; superficial disorder thus reveals its underlying order.

Representing earthly unity in diversity, *discordia concors* passed more or less intact from the Greek culture into the Roman, where again it is primarily cosmological, an attempt to describe the basic mechanism of the universe. Perhaps the most typical example is from Horace's *Epistles*:[13]

> Quae mare compescant causae, quid temperet annum,
> Stellae sponte sua iussaene vagentur et errent,
> Quid premat obscurum lunae, quid proferat orbem,
> Quid velit et possit rerum concordia discors.

Within the miraculous circle of the year, the four varying seasons are resolved, but the demarcation between the different seasons cannot be discerned, their confluence is so subtle. A sense of wonder and admiration fills this passage—that the orb of the moon slowly turns from darkness to light and back again to darkness in its endless cycle, that the stars wander out through the heavens but return each year, that the sea ebbs but turns on the tide. Mysteriously the discords of the world are harmonized into concord, containing the almost infinite diversity of nature, a view of *discordia concors* that also appears in such Roman authors as Ovid and Seneca.[14]

The apocryphal Book of Wisdom (11:20) contains the

formula used by medieval and Renaissance thinkers to bring classical theories of musical harmony within the compass of a Christian god, who "hast ordered all things in measure and number and weight." In *Of the Interchangeable Course, or Variety of Things in the Whole World* (London, 1594), Louis Le Roy offers a version of the Horatian use of *discordia concors* "to represent . . . the interchangeable course & alternation of all things in the world," which is but to mirror God's own method:

> I most humbly acknowledge the divine providence of God to be above all, beleeving assuredly, that God almighty, maker, and governour of this great worke so excellent in beauty, so admirable in varietie, and do singular in continuance . . . contayning in himselfe the beginning, the end, and the meanes of them all, and pursuing the order wh. he hath given the world, from the beginning in creating it, will that it be tempered by alternative chaunges, and maintayned by contraries, his eternall essence remayning alwaies one and unchangeable.

Through every stratum of life—"in the bodie of the world, . . . in mans bodie, . . . in the oeconomical bodie, . . . in the politike bodie"[15]—discords such as the four seasons are tempered and rendered into oneness by God's harmonizing spirit.[16]

If a gentle tempering of discords persists throughout corresponding bodies of the universe, a writer's poetry might well be expected to reflect similar tempering. Indeed, the "bodie" of art proves no exception, if one recalls the soft persuasion of Empedoclean Love, in which the quiet and mild contrast of various colors creates a harmonious composition:[17]

> And even as artists—men who know their craft
> Through wits of cunning—paint with streak and hue
> Bright temple-tablets, and will seize in hand
> The oozy poisons pied and red and gold
> (Mixing harmonious, now more, now less),
> From which they fashion forms innumerable,
> And like to all things, peopling a fresh world
> With trees, and men and women, beasts and birds.

During the Renaissance it was traditional to treat the arts, particularly landscape painting, as harmonious works composed of smaller, linked contasts. Contrast itself became an aesthetic ideal when widely held opinions on landscape painting expanded to include the sister arts,[18] as when E. K. applies the Horatian principle of *ut pictura poesis* to Spenser's "Shepheardes Calender":[19]

But all as in most exquisite pictures they use to blaze and portraict not onely the daintie lineaments of beautye, but also rounde about it to shadow the rude thickets and craggy clifts, that by the basenesse of such parts, more excellency may accrew to the principall; for oftimes we fynde ourselves, I knowe not how, singularly delighted with the shewe of such naturall rudenesse, and take great pleasure in that disorderly order. Even so doe those rough and harsh termes enlumine and make more clearly to appeare the brightnesse of brave and glorious words. So oftentimes a dischorde in Musick maketh a comely concordaunce.

The final allusion to the music in which concords are derived from discords only underlines the assumption that artistic excellence depends upon principles of contrast based ultimately in the idea of *discordia concors*.[20] Spenser's "Shepheardes Calender," for instance, is itself constructed upon such a model of a world that is oneness in multiplicity. Twelve months of four seasons vary within the confines of the circular year. In Milton's *Paradise Lost* the various voice of all creation praises God:[21]

> In mystic Dance not without Song, resound
> His praise, who out of Darkness call'd up Light.
> Air, and ye Elements the eldest birth
> Of Nature's Womb, that in quaternion run
> Perpetual Circle, multiform, and mix
> And nourish all things, let your ceaseless change
> Vary to our great Maker still new praise.

Like the four elements, disparate segments of the universe "run" in "Perpetual Circle," "in quaternion" or fours. The poet's art consciously imitates the *discordia concors* at the heart of nature—in its number, weight, and measure—because, as Lambert Daneau declares in *The Wonderfull Woorkmanship of the World* (London, 1578, fol. 86^r), it is God himself

who hath contempered all those thinges excellently one with another as they ought to bee, and hath made them of apt and convenient weight, number, and measure, both in respect of themselves, and in comparison also of other thinges, as it is written in the *booke of Wisdome.*

This principle of proportion had far-reaching effects upon poetry, since verse is literally and figuratively a composition of musical number and measure: "Harmonie is likewise number; so that the English verse then hath number, measure, and harmonie in the best proportion of Musicke."[22] In *Davideis* (1.33-40) Abraham Cowley petitions the muse to reveal the "mystick pow'ers" of "blest *Numbers*" that he might also imitate "*Gods Poem*, this *Worlds* new *Essay*," and like God, bring nature's "ungovern'd parts" "to *Number* and fixt Rules" and so create a "measur'd *Dance* of *All*." Emulating, in similar fashion, the cosmic "*Harmonie*" of *discordia concors*, which "*Gods Breath* did tunefully inspire," the shepherd-poet David "did *Sauls* wild rage controul. / And tun'd the harsh disorders of his *Soul*."[23] A poem built upon *discordia concors* as unity in multiplicity is thus a reflection of the Creator's providential pattern.[24] All differences are contained within God's unifying essence, as Cowley asserts ("Ode: Of Wit," st. 8):

> In a true piece of *Wit* all things must be,
> Yet all things there *agree*.

Gradually the Renaissance moved from an ideal of simple unity in multiplicity toward the aesthetic of stark contrariety, so characteristic of metaphysical wit. The gradual change in emphasis may be seen in E. K.'s comment on Spenser's style. E. K. delighted in the "disorderly order" created when "rough and harsh termes enlumine and make more clearly to appeare the brightnesse of brave and glorious words." It is the actual placement of the words themselves that composes an admirable contrast between light and dark. In Orazio Lombardelli's discourse on Tasso's *Gerusalemme liberata*, there is heightened interest in the actual poetic process of overcoming the resistance of diverse elements of plot and structure to unification. The more difficult to fuse discords into concord, the more cause for wonder and applause at its achievement:[25]

the marvelous chain of all the actions grafted on to the main one with those marvelous connections . . . that he should have succeeded so well in knotting and tying all the parts of this poem of his . . . to have promised to sing the glorious reconquest, and then to have delayed it so much, to have put so many things in its way, to have interrupted it, and to have brought it almost to the point of desperation . . . and with so much verisimilitude, and interweaving, and correspondence of one part with another that there are never any doubts of importance remaining and that the memory is never so disturbed that it would fail to attach quickly one thing to another; until at the end all the obstacles give way.

The very difficulty of joining "one part with another" and the pleasure derived from subduing "all the obstacles" suggests that we are not very far from Dr. Johnson's description of metaphysical wit "as a kind of *discordia concors*," in which "the most heterogeneous ideas are yoked by violence together."

The interpretation of *discordia concors* as a violent yoking of opposites proved more suited to the spirit of seventeenth-century England which, according to Michael Radau in the *Orator extemporaneus* (London, 1673), was sickened by the simplicity of so much ordinary writing, preferring the complexities of wit (*acumen*) exemplified by *discordia concors*:[26]

Nauseat simplicitatem seculum nostrum, & . . . in stylo luxum requirit. . . . Loquamur itaque de Acuto, ut seculo nos accommodemus. . . . Sicut materiale Acumen est duarum linearum seu duorum laterum in unum punctum concursus . . . : ita Acumen metaphoricum est concursus seu discors concordia *Subjecti + Praedicati* in oratione. . . . Acumen est concors discordia, seu discors concordia.

Radau's final equation of wit with *discordia concors* is a commonplace in the seventeenth century. We find, for example, John Newton's recommendation in *The Art of Rhetorick* (London, 1671) that orators adopt the "Metaphorical sharpness" created by a "disagreeing concord" or "agreeing discord" (p. 28).

A striking parallel to the "sharpness" of metaphysical wit exists in the antique cosmologies of Greece and Rome where, for instance, Heraclitus believed that the world was built upon "integrated contrasts," wherein "harmony dominates, but, a harmony which comprehends strife and antagonism."[27] And because the tendency toward concord is always countered by the tendency toward discord, an uneasy tension results from the "bending back" of the Heraclitean bow or lyrestring: "People do not understand how that which is at variance with itself agrees with itself. There is a harmony in the bending back, as in the case of the bow and the lyre."[28] *Discordia concors* embraces all such contraries that harmoniously correspond while they oppose one another. The Roman poet Manilius divined the same fundamental yoking of opposite elements within the universe:[29]

> Applying Hot to Cold, to Humid Dry.
> To Heavy Light, which kind Discordancy
> The Matrimonial Bands of Nature Knits,
> And Principles for all Production fits;
> We can but guess its Birth: obscur'd it lies
> Beyond the reach of Men and Deities.

Like the bow of Heraclitus, the clash of opposites characterizes the wit of secular metaphysical verse, where it creates a dynamic tension between the terms of the *discordia concors* that is neither transcended nor resolved. In religious poetry, on the other hand, a new element emerges, the yoking of opposites that attempts to reconcile the contrarieties and paradoxes of earthly life by transcending them.

Since there is, however, no classical precedent for resolving contrariety in God, the motivation to launch the soul beyond this world through a violent yoking of opposites springs, at least in part, from changes in sixteenth- and seventeenth-century England. As the gentle blending of discords under the direction of a benevolent Creator seemed to disappear, the emotional distance widened between the ideal and actual, the physical and spiritual, the visible and invisible, the secular and religious. Steadily the suspicion intensified that earth no longer reflected the perfection of heaven.[30] Poetry based upon unity in multiplicity was therefore unable to harmonize the radical disjunction between earth and heaven. Such a divorce had profound effects upon art, as we can see in Donne's *First Anniversary*: "What Artist now dares boast that he can bring/ Heaven hither . . . The art is lost, and correspondence too."[31]

The Historical Tradition

During this divisive period the metaphysical writers seem to have found the philosophical concept of *discordia concors* as a yoking of opposites expressive of their own disturbingly discordant world. Once apprehended as a cosmic model—"such things as before were divers and different, do accord and agree together, to establish, intertain, and embellish one an other, the contrarietie, becoming unitie; and the discord concord; the enmitie amitie; and contention covenant"—the idea itself became the means to create an entirely new and vigorous literary style.[32] And depending upon their purposes, either the wit of *discordia concors* might mirror extreme tensions within daily life, or when *discordia concors* itself failed to organize and resolve earthly contrariety, poets might turn to the concept as a means of spiritual transcendence. Since Christianity has traditionally been written in paradox—one loses his life to gain it, the meek shall inherit the earth, the last shall come first—the paradox of *discordia concors* naturally suggests itself as the basic mode of expression in religious verse.

So difficult was it to assert truths set forth easily in the Middle Ages when a system of correspondences lent design and coherence to the world, that in the earlier phase of metaphysical wit especially, poets deliberately imitated the very difficulties they experienced in rejoining what had grown not merely dissimilar but now altogether contrary. Later in the century, however, difficulty becomes impossibility, and even *discordia concors* is completely unable to yoke "the most heterogeneous ideas . . . by violence together" to resolve contrariety, thus necessitating the reemergence at mid-century of *discordia concors* as unity in multiplicity, whose purpose is now also transcendent, but which emphasizes the acceptance of discord until the work of time restores man to concord and paradise. These distinctions between different kinds of *discordia concors* serve effectively as working definitions and prove useful in reading metaphysical poetry, but the concept informs the wit of each poet in such varied ways that the lines tend, of course, to blur in the poetry itself.

TWO

JOHN DONNE: YOKING OF OPPOSITES

The profound disjunction between the world of nature and the world of spirit so pervasive in seventeenth-century England may be witnessed in Donne's *Songs and Sonnets*, the verse most typically considered "metaphysical." Although human love is the theme of the series, no consistent philosophy of love unifies the collection. The great variety of attitudes expressed in Donne's secular lyrics may perhaps be best characterized by *discordia concors*, wherein the poet attempts to reconcile opposites, especially those of body and soul, sense and spirit. When such opposites meet, however, they either clash violently and resist resolution, or they achieve a paradoxical resolution without transcendence of the body.

Numerous poems, such as "Womans Constancy" and "The Dampe," imply that the desire for sexual gratification is the man's primary concern. In "The Dampe," for example, Donne exhibits extreme impatience with the restraining conventions of courtly love—the constancy of the lady to her "enchantresse *Honor*" and the constancy of the man to perpetually pursue her—finally demanding that they discard their courtly roles and simply make love as man and woman:[1]

> Kill mee as Woman, let mee die
> As a meere man; doe you but try
> Your passive valor, and you shall finde than,
> Naked you'have odds enough of any man.

John Donne: Yoking of Opposites

The lover proposes that rather than kill him by her constancy, the lady should subdue her false conventions, "disdaine" and "honor," and "kill" him sexually instead. Donne hopes that his passionate fervor and sexual frustration will circumvent the fundamentally paradoxical situation generated by the very nature of courtly love poetry, in which physical consummation rarely occurs if each partner remains faithful to the rules. Since the man's goal, sex, is opposite to the women's, honor, an inherent tension permeates these poems.[2] What distinguishes Donne's seductions is the manner in which he seeks to outwit (by wit) the traditional stalemate. In "The Flea," for instance, the poet wins our incredulous admiration through a series of outrageously illogical, and finally amusing, analogies. Since this flea has already bitten both of us, Donne intones with mock-seriousness, "This flea is you and I, and this / Our mariage bed, and mariage temple is," then obviously they are already married and so why not make love? Leaving no time for one to linger upon the absurdity of such a definition of marriage, Donne renews his proposition, announcing if the lady dares to kill the flea (which she gamely does), then she is desecrating their marriage temple. And, if she takes the flea's death so lightly, well, then, that is just how inconsequential her honor will seem, so she should therefore amiably acquiesce to his desire.[3]

"Loves Alchymie" demonstrates how difficult it is to consider love as ennobling, for somehow the body must be converted into spirit. Although the speaker boasts that he has "lov'd, and got, and told," the mystery of love has remained elusive. Those who swear it is platonic merely pretend to hear the harmony of the spheres. The marriage ritual is viewed as an attempt to elevate sex and spiritualize the physical aspect of love, but the endeavor is as false as the alchemists who brag over their "pregnant pot" when, in fact, the elixir that will transmute base metals into gold is yet undiscovered. The poet of course implies that as an elixir love, too, has failed to transmute the base metal of body into the gold of spiritual love. For the alchemist to rhapsodize over "Some odoriferous thing, or med'cinall" is analogous to those lovers who "dreame a rich and long delight, / But get a winter-seeming summers night." Love of women, in the speaker's opinion, is "imposture all." "Hope not for minde in women," he declares; "at their best / Sweetnesse and wit, they' are but *Mummy,* possest." Since restorative powers were then attributed to a preserved corpse, physical possession of the woman relieves the man temporarily. Mummy is, however, dead flesh. Sexual appetite in this context is therefore equivalent to necrophilia. Taking the woman bodily ironically reminds the man of his own mortality. The female form may be likened to a death's head, a *memento mori.* Love does raise one heavenward—not platonically as the marriage partners feign—but as a reminder of one's ultimate death. There is no hint in "Loves Alchymie" that love is either spiritually ennobling or emotionally transcendent.

The opening lines of "Aire and Angels" auspiciously suggest that Donne has discovered spiritual love:[4]

> Twice or thrice had I lov'd thee,
> Before I knew thy face or name;
> So in a voice, so in a shapelesse flame,
> Angells affect us oft, and worship'd bee.

As angels were thought to invisibly affect people, so the idea of a woman whom he has never seen entrances Donne. Readers justifiably expect a disquisition on spiritual love to follow. After all, the poet has just confessed he worships a woman whose body he has yet to even glimpse. But despite the positive tone and the positive expectations they arouse, the first four lines are expressed negatively. The ostensible compliment is further qualified when Donne meets the lady, whom he then ambiguously terms a "lovely glorious nothing." Either she has shattered his original fantasies, or she *is* lovely, but that is "nothing."

The poet then argues, with logic resembling the conclusion of "The Extasie," that since his soul has created a "child," that is, his notion that he loves the woman, the idea must now also take physical form: "Love must not be, but take a body too." Donne was not above laughing at himself, for the sly sexual innuendoes in the preceeding line soon backfire. When the "lovely glorious nothing" becomes something, the poet's admiration is so occupied that rather than increasing, curiously has the opposite and, I find, humorous effect of exhausting him:

> Whilst thus to ballast love, I thought,
>   And so more steddily to have gone,
> With wares which would sinke admiration,
> I saw, I had loves pinnace overfraught,
>   Ev'ry thy haire for love to worke upon
> Is much too much.

Worn out from excessive physical indulgence, and from the minute admiration of the lady's every hair, Donne decides that love itself cannot "inhere" "in nothing, nor in things / Extreme," so that as the "shapelesse flame" was too insubstantial, conversely, physical love proves too weighty. The perception of love as spiritual was thus immediately countered by its opposite. The tenuous conclusion of the poem reflects a *discordia concors* that consists of[5]

> Just such disparitie
> As is twixt Aire and Angells puritie,
> 'Twixt womens love, and mens will ever bee.

It is finally difficult to decide whether Donne here believes love of women to be an experience comparably angelic; not altogether disagreeable; or definitely pleasant.

Although "The Undertaking" is a lesser poem than "The Extasie" or "The Canonization," its previously underestimated complexity provides an excellent example of Donne's recurring interest in the tension that exists between spiritual and physical love.

After boasting of "one braver thing / Then all the *Worthies* did"—the capacity to detect "lovelinesse within" a woman—the speaker invites his hypothetical listener to imitate his undertaking:

> If, as I have, you also doe
>   Vertue'attir'd in woman see,
> And dare love that, and say so too,
>   And forget the Hee and Shee;
> And if this love, though placed so,
>   From prophane men you hide,
> Which will no faith on this bestow,
>   Or, if they doe, deride.

Since, however, there is only one woman in the world so splendid ("no more / Such stuffe to worke upon, there is"), the tone of "The Undertaking" is, I think, unmistakably double-edged, with cynicism accompanying every bravado overture to spiritual love. If forgetting the "Hee and Shee" may be taken as a definition of spiritual love,[6] an earthly approximation of the neutral state of love reputedly enjoyed by angels, the speaker's own cynicism simultaneously pulls our responses in the opposite direction, so that a *discordia concors* of yoked but unresolved contraries is created. It is not, after all, the assertion of loving virtue that makes profane men suspicious and earns their derision, it is the claim that love for a woman is love of virtue. The consequence is the paradox of the poem—keep love hidden. In other words, avoid its bodily manifestation. To keep love hidden is to abstain from sex, to "forget the Hee and Shee." Heterosexual love, from the speaker's rather cynical point of view, is thus redeemed by annihilating it.

Without becoming overly entangled in the web of critical commentary surrounding "The Extasie,"[7] I think it fair to say that however one interprets the poem, problems remain because, as in "The Undertaking," unresolved paradox again constitutes the central issue. In "The Extasie," however, the situation is reversed, and it is spiritual love that must descend to bodies and there be revealed (65-72):

> So must pure lovers soules descend
>   T'affections, and to faculties,
> That sense may reach and apprehend,
>   Else a great Prince in prison lies.
>
> To'our bodies turne wee then, that so
>   Weake men on love reveal'd may looke;
> Loves mysteries in soules doe grow,
>   But yet the body is his booke.

The paradoxes of hiding and revealing love create a rather ambiguous tone that oscillates between "refin'd" seriousness and varying degrees of cynicism and drollery.

Unlike the several poems that express either failure to attain mutual love or to reconcile the bodily and spiritual, many of Donne's finest lyrics, such as "The Good-morrow," "The Canonization," and "The Sunne Rising," celebrate a mutually pleasurable love experience. In "The Sunne Rising," for instance, it cannot be said that the poet is attempting to transcend the body, for the poem itself is a hip-hip-hooray for physical love. In fact, the argument offered negates the necessity for transcendence: "She' is all States, and all Princes, I, / Nothing else is." The wit depends upon the paradox that the lovers encompass the entire world—"All here in one bed lay"—for it is this declaration that controls the "unruly Sunne" of the first line. The diurnal sun that wakes and disturbs the sleep of ordinary lovers—and the fleeting time it represents—is converted into a symbol of eternity through the poem's assertion that the lovers are the world itself. The sun therefore neither rises nor sets on their love. Since the sun's "duties" are

> To warme the world, that's done in warming us.
> Shine here to us, and thou art every where;
> This bed thy center is, these walls, thy spheare.

Both time and their love are rendered unchanging. The paradox that "all" is "one" now makes good Donne's earlier definition of love:

> Love, all alike, no season knowes, nor clyme,
> Nor houres, dayes, months, which are the rags of time.

There is no need to transcend the world; the lovers embody it.[8]

The wit of all the *Songs and Sonnets* may be characterized by the manner in which human love itself reflects a kind of *discordia concors*, a harmony of dissonant emotions. When, through the tortuous wit of Donne's metaphysical conceits, the love of the man and his lady became a microcosm, it was world enough, but the poet's sacred verse betrays perhaps an additional strain because here the world itself comes between the poet and God, the object of his affection, like those "Iron wedges" in Marvell's "Definition of Love." In Donne's devotional works, therefore, he employs *discordia concors* not merely to mirror the harmonious tension between contrary emotions, but to be the dynamic means of translating the earthly into an apprehension of the heavenly.

If the Middle Ages readily discovered God's metaphors in the world at large, then familiarly called the Book of Nature, the seventeenth century increasingly failed to perceive divine pattern there. Rather than view nature as a series of causally related events as science does, the medieval mind finds connections between things based not upon cause and effect but upon similitude, a tendency which led to the "symbolist attitude" of the Middle Ages. The world itself became, as Johan Huizinga points out, a repository of "correlated figures" of the divine.[9] Free from the restricting confines of thinking causally, the medieval mind roved at will—laterally, vertically, simultaneously—seeing intimations of the heavenly in the humblest of God's creations. The cross-piece inside a walnut shell might, for instance, lead the mind to dwell upon the Crucifixion, but this association only possesses symbolic potential when it is assumed that their common attributes are both "essential" (in philosophical terms), and, as such, "real" entities. The belief that the walnut shares the essence of the Crucifixion brings the mind at once to contemplate the heavenly. As men increasingly came to fear, however, that nature might contain only particulars—the unique (e. g., an individual walnut) divorced from its possible symbolic associations—the spiritual, the divine, and the deity himself, receded from earthly view. Sir Thomas Browne thus aptly defines seventeenth-century man as that "great and true *Amphibium*," who lives "in divided and distinguished worlds."[10]

Browne's perception that "we are onely that amphibious piece betweene a corporall and spirituall essence, that middle forme that linkes those two together, and makes good the method of God and nature, that jumps not from extreames, but unites the incompatible distances, by some middle and participating natures" (*R.M.* 1.34) illuminates the manner whereby *discordia concors* becomes the means for spiritual transcendence. To effect a transition from the earthly to the heavenly, the poet must detect those mediating terms that join extremes.

The mediating position that Browne assigns to man in the universe is filled in poetics by metaphor. Since metaphor always asserts both sameness and difference, it can work in two opposite directions at once. This distinctive quality singles metaphor out as the mediating term between heaven and earth, but as will become evident, only conceptual and divine metaphors can span such vast distances.

By the time Donne was composing his lyrics, metaphor had changed from its traditional role, in which it dressed concepts with words, to one in which it dressed words with concepts.[11] Formerly, metaphor was simply one of several available rhetorical devices used to amplify, embellish—dress up—an idea, so that in effect its function had been to illustrate, decorate, or make ideas perspicuous. Ideas, on the other hand, were considered independently of their verbal embroidery. When metaphor assumed new prominence, however, it became a fit vehicle for metaphysical verse, whose thoughts are inseparably enmeshed with their form and expression.

Originally poetic "invention" was thought to be the "discovery" of God's metaphors that readily lay at hand in his two Books of Nature and of Scripture. When, however, skepticism had sufficiently undermined faith that images of the divine were immanent in visible nature, the source of metaphor's mediating function shifted more directly to the metaphysical poet's wit, which, in imitation of God, the first artist, now conceives, rather than merely finds, metaphors which assert an essential truth—analogous to God's reality, if not identical to it.[12] Creation of such "conceptual" metaphors initially disturbs the poet, however, for how is he to know that his metaphors are analogous to God's? Further, are they demonic or divine? And most importantly, are they capable of asserting "essential" truths, for only such metaphors can draw the mind upwards to meditate upon God. To bridge the gap between earth and distant heaven thus depends upon wit's creation of metaphors that are both conceptual and divine. Although Donne and Herbert employ Scripture differently, its role now becomes increasingly critical to each, for biblical metaphors can reliably confirm that the poet's are also divine. When, for instance, Herbert describes the miseries of his life, he cannot find peace until Scripture transforms and validates his metaphors ("The H. Scriptures II"):

>Thy words do finde me out, & parallels bring,
>And in another make me understood.

Once Herbert sees his own life in terms of biblical metaphor, his metaphors are assured of their essential truth. In this fashion contradiction is resolved, and suddenly, "Grief melts away / Like snow in May" ("The Flower" 5-6). Similar assurance is granted to Donne in "A Hymne to Christ, at the Authors last going into Germany,"[13] when God's metaphors assuage the poet's fear of drowning (1-4):

>In what torne ship soever I embarke,
>That ship shall be my embleme of thy Arke;
>What sea soever swallow mee, that flood
>Shall be to mee an embleme of thy blood.

For every earthly ship there is an answer in God's eternal "arke"; for every "sea" that drowns, there is God's saving "blood." Thus full of faith Donne sets off from England, trusting that although he has been divided from all he loves at home, God may save him (11-12):

>When I have put our seas twixt them and mee,
>Put thou thy sea betwixt my sinnes and thee.

In their essential likeness to God's metaphors, man's are confirmed. With this knowledge Donne joyously declares in the final stanza (25-32):

>Seale then this bill of my Divorce to all,
>On whom those fainter beames of love did fall;
>Marry those loves, which in youth scattered bee
>On Fame, Wit, Hopes (false mistresses) to thee.
>Churches are best for Prayer, that have least light:
>To see God only, I goe out of sight:
>>And to scape stormy dayes, I chuse
>>An Everlasting night.

Despite his separation from family, friends, and country, the poet believes that God can "marry" all earthly divorces and make all earthly metaphors divine. Thus, imitating God, Donne yokes opposites together: he chooses churches with "least light," "to see God only" he goes "out of sight," and to escape "stormy dayes," he chooses "everlasting night." Donne yokes such opposites together in the faith that God's metaphors answer and perfect every discord, that in eternity God has already married all divorces.

From Donne's *Devotions upon Emergent Occasions* we may deduce more precisely how in metaphysical verse the conceptual and divine metaphor mediates between heaven and earth:[14]

But wherefore, O my God, hast thou presented to us the afflictions and calamities of this life in the name of waters? so often in the name of waters, and deep waters, and seas of waters? Must we look to be drowned? are they bottomless, are they boundless? That is not the dialect of thy language; thou hast given a remedy against the deepest water by water; against the inundation of sin by baptism; and the first life that thou gavest to any creatures was in waters: therefore thou dost not threaten us with an irremediableness when affliction is a sea.

Two metaphors are set forth above. In the first, "afflictions" are compared to "deep waters," and in the second, the "remedy" is also likened to water. Although opposites, both metaphors share the common attribute of water, but "afflictions" is an imperfect, incomplete, visible, earthly metaphor—seen from the aspect of time, while the cure is seen from the aspect of eternity, and is God's full and perfect metaphor. Thus, in nearly all metaphysical verse there is a strain between the two kinds of metaphor, the earthly and the divine. The strain to convert or transmute earthly metaphor into its divine counterpart is typical of the difficulty faced in secular and religious poetry. Only faith permits the poet to see beyond the horizon of the visible, to see that all which appears incomplete and imperfect in the world is completed and perfected in God: "The assurance of future mercy is present mercy" (*Devotions*, p. 129). It is this "present" "assurance" that permits divine metaphor to span earth and heaven. For example, from a temporal point of view, "affliction" is a "sea," but from the perspective of eternity the very opposite is true—the red sea is "the sea of thy Son's blood" that cures all ills (p. 127). Even should afflictions prove too deep a sea, God is an ark come to save mankind: "Thou hast made a way in the sea, and a safe path in the waters, showing that thou canst save from all dangers" (ibid.). Mortal, visible, earthly, transient circumstances predominate in nature, but Scripture duplicates an aspect of those circumstances, which confirms that the poet's metaphors are true and not demonic. And because an essential relationship between the earthly and heavenly can be discovered in Scripture, contraries may be united. Scripture thus reanimates the external world with spirit. Nature itself becomes alive with God's metaphors because, to echo Sir Thomas Browne, "reason" (wit) has discovered the "invisible" realms of faith (*R.M.* 1.34).

Since all God's creations are metaphorical, it is possible to join dissimilars once the proper perspective is gained. Metaphor is an intrinsic attribute of God himself: "How often, how much more often," declares Donne in the *Devotions*, "doth thy Son call himself a way, and a light, and a gate, and a vine, and bread, than the Son of God, or of man? How much oftener doth he exhibit a metaphorical Christ, than a real, a literal?" (p. 125). To reunite dissimilars Donne imitates the metaphorical style of the Holy Ghost, which (pp. 125-26)

> hath occasioned thine ancient servants, whose delight it was to write after thy copy, to proceed the same way in their expositions of the Scriptures, and in their composing both of public liturgies and of private prayers to thee, to make their accesses to thee in such a kind of language as thou wast pleased to speak to them, in a figurative, in a metaphorical language.

Donne seeks the same inspiration that guided God's "ancient servants"; he seeks to find a validation of his poetic metaphors in their correspondence to God's own "copy."

At least three kinds of strain pervade metaphysical verse. In secular poetry one observes a growing violence as poets attempt to force "the most heterogeneous ideas" together.

But resolution is not achieved; contraries remain in violent juxtaposition and continual strife. The tension that results is the *discordia concors* represented by the bow of Heraclitus, whose harmony is born of endless discord. Such strain is characteristic of secular verse in the early 1600s, and is especially evident in Donne's *Songs and Sonnets*. In their religious poetry, however, the metaphysicals displayed a second kind of strain or violence, exemplified by the "waters" that are either "afflictions" or "remedies." Such contrariety and conflicting emotion may be resolved by wit's creation through *discordia concors* of divine metaphors that successfully transform the imperfections and failures of earthly metaphor. But even divine metaphor itself betrays a special strain of its own as it attempts transcendence. The varieties of strain in devotional poetry abound in Donne's two *Anniversaries*.

The *Anniversaries* themselves are extremely difficult poems, and have been variously interpreted.[15] Donne purports to ritually celebrate and re-create the death of a young girl, Elizabeth Drury. Since, however, Donne scarcely knew the child and hoped to gain patronage from her father, his praise has often been called extravagant and inappropriate. Many critics have thus argued that it must be some other, more worthy figure that Donne eulogizes. Marjorie Nicolson, for example, proposes the Virgin Mary, Queen Elizabeth I, and Astraea, the goddess of justice who forsook earth for heaven when nature became so decayed. Manley sees Elizabeth Drury as representative of *sapientia* or wisdom. Even Ben Jonson in his "Conversations . . . with Drummond" (1619) grumbles that had the *Anniversaries* been about the "Virgin Marie" it would have been a worthy endeavor, but Donne's own reply that he "described the Idea of a Woman and not as she was" is meant precisely.[16] Elizabeth Drury is the "subject" and the "object" of the *Anniversaries*—both "accidentally" as she herself, and "essentially" as she represents the "Idea" of "Woman." Her death becomes the means of symbolizing the death and chaos of the world, wrought by the Fall of Eve, first woman. And simultaneously it becomes the means of foreshadowing the restoration of all, through Christ, born of Mary, second Eve. Thus, what appears hyperbolical in Donne's praise of Elizabeth Drury is true. Meditation upon her death and her goodness may "cal" us after her, upwards to heaven where all the dead are revived.

To achieve that spiritual transcendence, Donne seeks to convert the earthly and imperfect metaphors of *The First Anniversary* into the divine and "wholesome" metaphors of *The Second Anniversary*. The poetic strategy of demonstrating division before revealing its opposite is typical both of the *Anniversaries* and the sermons. The full title of the first poem—"An / Anatomy / Of the World. / Wherein, / By Occasion of / The Untimely Death of Mistris / Elizabeth Drury / The Frailty and the Decay / Of This Whole World / Is Represented"—indicates that an "anatomy" or dissection shall be performed on the "body" of the ailing world to determine the cause of its illness, but as shall later become evident, metaphor, poetic structure, and theme also undergo the same "anatomy." As the world's frailty and Elizabeth's death lead men to question the axioms of the ages, the poet begins the necessary first process of fragmentation. On the cosmic scale (*F.A.* 205-14)[17]

> new Philosophy cals all in doubt,
> The Element of fire is quite put out;
> The Sunne is lost, and th'earth, and no man's wit
> Can well direct him, where to looke for it.
> And freely men confesse, that this world's spent,
> When in the Planets, and the Firmament
> They seeke so many new; they see that this
> Is crumbled out againe to his Atomis.
> 'Tis all in pieces, all cohaerence gone;
> All just supply, and all Relation.

Not only is *The First Anniversary* an example of the commonplace theme of *contemptus mundi*, but Donne is also undoubtedly reacting to the increasing anxiety that external nature no longer reflected a divine pattern, which if true would bar "commerce twixt heaven and earth" (*F.A.* 399).[18] Exiled from heaven, seventeenth-century poets faced a crisis in art and in life (*F.A.* 391-92, 396):

> What Artist now dares boast that he can bring
> Heaven hither . . .
>
> * * *
>
> The art is lost, and correspondence too.

The distance between earth and heaven is becoming almost too great to span. In *The Second Part of the French Academie* (London, 1605) Pierre de la Primaudaye analyzes the difficulty of comprehending God under such circumstances:[19]

> For if wee cannot comprehend the creature, or the nature thereof how shall wee comprehende that of the creatour? Jesus Christ saide to *Nichodemus, If when I tell you earthly things, yee beleeve not, howe should yee beleeve, if I tell you of heavenly things?* We may say the like heere, that if it be impossible for us thoroughly to know the earth, or the body or soule of man, or the nature and vertue thereof, how shall wee know the heavens and spirituall natures, or God and his woorkes? For if it be beyond our reach to discerne them in our selves . . . how shall we comprehend his workes in the whole world?

By the close of *The First Anniversary* heaven and earth appear to be completely divided: "Heaven keepes soules, / The grave keeps bodies" (*F.A.* 473-74). Donne, however, makes careful allusions to the connection that exists not only between the spiritual and the mundane worlds, but between the two *Anniversaries* themselves, for he prefaces the above lines by pointedly noting that poetry "hath a middle nature" (*F.A.* 473). He also chides readers who consider Elizabeth's praises "as matter fit for Chronicle, not verse" (*F.A.* 460) and reminds us (*F.A.* 461-66)

> that God did make
> A last, and lastingst peece, a song. He spake
> To *Moses,* to deliver unto all,
> That song: because he knew they would let fall,
> The Law, the Prophets, and the History,
> But keepe the song still in their memory.

At the verge of the promised land that he never enters, Moses delivers his bitter song to the Chosen People (Deut. 31: 19-30), for he knows they will "let fall" the covenant and the Law. Moses' song thus at once betokens a world in "peeces" like that in *The First Anniversary* and the paradise to come, a sight glimpsed by readers in *The Second Anniversary*. Donne's reference to Moses' song at the very end of the first poem suggests that it is related to *The Second Anniversary* in the same way that the Old and New Testaments are to each other: the Old foreshadows the New as the first poem prefigures the second.[20] Both poems thus compose a two-part harmony: Moses' song adumbrates the New Testament "song" of Christ, the *carmen musicum*, [21] and it is Christ who will reconcile the old law of justice and the new law of mercy, as well as harmonize the "peeces" of the anatomized world. Boldly invading the "great Office" of biblical prophet (*F.A.* 468), the poet himself becomes God's trumpet—at first to awaken and warn his people against the world disordered by sin, but then to proclaim the New Testament song of grace—that all men might become *carmen musicum*, true music, true harmony. In *The Second Anniversary* Donne explicitly reveals his role as prophet when he declares that Elizabeth "shouldest for life, and death, a patterne bee" (*S.A.* 524, 527-28):

> Thou art the Proclamation; and I ame
> The Trumpet, at whose voice the people came.

Imitating God, Donne frames the "patterne" of Elizabeth's life and death "in due measure" (*F.A.* 467) of poetic song. And, in so far as she is the "Idea of a Woman," the essence of Mary, second Eve, Elizabeth's is a mediating role. Contemplation of her death brings an ecstatic vision of the bliss to come, when we too join the heavenly "quire" ("Praise of the Dead" 35-48, *F.A.* 10) and exchange Elizabeth's song for Christ's. Similarly, "verse hath a middle nature" (*F.A.* 473), for it mediates between apparent opposites, heaven and earth.

The reunion of earth with heaven is achieved by the poet's change of perspective. From "below," amidst the fragments and pieces of the dissection, "small things seeme great" (*S.A.* 293, 294). Looking through such "spectacles," one sees but the imperfect, broken body of the world, but to see these pieces as an adumbration of heaven, the poet must exchange his temporal and partial vision of things, for an eternal and perfect perspective (*S.A.* 294-300)

>   But up unto the watch-towre get,
> And see all things despoyled of fallacies:
> Thou shalt not peepe through lattices of eies,
> Nor heare through Laberinths of eares, nor learne
> By circuit, or collections to discerne.
> In Heaven thou straight know'st all, concerning it,
> And what concerns it not, shall straight forget.

From high above in the "watch-towre" the poet looks down on earth and sees at last how all the broken and fragmented pieces fit. By changing his perspective from an earthly and imperfect speculation to an eternal one, he understands that God does have a place for all the "peeces" within his providential pattern.

The proper attitude toward the "fragmentary rubbidge" (*S.A.* 82) of a dying world is to "Thinke then, My soule, that death is but a Groome / Which brings a Taper to the outward roome" (*S.A.* 85-86). The "death" of the world and of man (as it was for Elizabeth) is a prelude to life in heaven: "For such approches doth Heaven make in death" (*S.A.* 89). As Moses prophesied in his song that men would "let fall" the Laws, and as "Solomon" foretold in Ecclesiastes 12 that the world would first be shaken into pieces, so we must remember that such destruction is but the "approch" to the harmony of a new heaven and earth. Similarly, the sooner one dies, the sooner one escapes earthly imperfection to join heaven's "quire." In these tortured poetic maneuvers Donne begins to turn Elizabeth's death into its opposite. The poet then directs his own soul to imitate a dying man (*S.A.* 90-92):

> Thinke thy selfe laboring now with broken breath,
> And thinke those broken and soft Notes to bee
> Division, and thy happiest Harmonee.

The labored, "broken breath" is likened to musical notes, which are in turn specified as "division" and "happiest Harmonee." "Division" usually refers to discord or separation, but in the Renaissance "division" also denoted its own opposite, "harmony." Etymologically "harmony" simply means "to fit together," but musically it refers to the concord created when various notes are combined. More particularly, "division" signifies the breaking of long musical notes into shorter ones that are then played rapidly. In this poetic context the pun on "division" reaffirms Donne's argument that the fragmentation of earthly life is but the first step to the "harmonee" of heaven. The faster the disintegration, the sooner paradise may be entered. When properly regarded from the aspect of eternity, the pun on "division," one can now appreciate, refers—as the biblical prophets foretold—to shaking the world into pieces in *The First Anniversary* and to "happiest Harmonee" in *The Second Anniversary*. By "such approches" Donne finally reveals destruction and death as the twin of their opposites.

But the conversion of death into life is not yet complete. At "Gods great Venite" (*S.A.* 44) the body's "labored breath" must cease altogether. Then, as Elizabeth's was, the soul will be freed to fly to heaven. Repeatedly the exhortation to "thinke" punctuates *The Second Anniversary*, but it is an exhortation to think in the cheerful light of faith (*S.A.* 184-89):

> Thinke thy sheell broke, thinke thy Soule hatch'd but now.
> And thinke this slow-pac'd soule, which late did cleave,
> To'a body, and went but by the bodies leave,
> Twenty, perchance, or thirty mile a day,
> Dispatches in a minute all the way,
> Twixt Heaven, and Earth.

As his mind follows Elizabeth Drury's soul in its flight "through the Firmament" (*S.A.* 206), past the very stars that once glittered like so many beads scattered at random, Donne perceives universal design (*S.A.* 207-13):

> And as these stars were but so many beades
> Strunge on one string, speed undistinguish'd leades
> Her through those spheares, as through the beades, a string,
> Whose quicke succession makes it still one thing:
> As doth the Pith, which, least our Bodies slack,
> Strings fast the little bones of necke, and backe;
> So by the soule doth death string Heaven and Earth.

Speeding through the "spheares," the mind loses its former earth-bound perspective. The actual celerity, the "quicke succession," integrates and orders the once discrete segments of the "firmament" so that suddenly they become "one thing." Here especially the very purpose of *discordia concors* is to apprehend just such a transcendent state in which seeming opposites are "yoked by violence together." Donne's soul tastes heavenly bliss once he has seen that the imperfect earthly metaphors "below" are transformed and fulfilled by God, if rightly regarded.

The "stars" that "were but so many beades / Strunge on one string" suggests the image of a chain of beads, but some of the terms are left unspecified. A sense of mystery shrouds the connection between the sections; the reader himself must "thinke" if he, too, is to follow the flight of Elizabeth's soul. The "string" that links the beads, for instance, performs several functions. Like the stars, and the bones of the spinal column, remote heaven and earth also require "string" if they are to be reunited. It is the "soule" that must "string" these opposites together. When the chain is completed, earth is joined with heaven once more. Paradoxically, however, for the soul to yoke heaven and earth, "death must usher, and unlocke the doore" (*S.A.* 156). Death must release the soul by unstringing it from the body so that it may soar straight to heaven (*S.A.* 93-95):

> Thinke thee laid on thy death bed, loose and slacke;
> And thinke that but unbinding of a packe,
> To take one precious thing, thy soule, from thence.

When death unbinds the body, the soul "strings fast" the way to heaven. Speeding upwards through the universe, the soul ties all the remote "peeces" of worldly life into "one thing"— one coherent pattern. By changing from an earthly to a divine perspective, the two contraries, heaven and earth, are yoked together. Donne restores life to the cut-up, anatomized body of the world, and he has accomplished this resuscitation through *discordia concors*, a yoking of opposites, whose purpose is transcendent.

The strain to convert the poet's own earthly metaphor to divine, in order to achieve an ecstatic embrace between a divided heaven and earth, is not only deliberate but peculiarly characteristic of Donnean wit. But for Donne there is an additional strain to make divine metaphor itself work. In *The Second Anniversary*, for instance, we must deduce that the metaphor of a chain is latently present. Further, Donne mimetically imitates the strain of creating divine metaphor by intentionally separating the several aspects of the chain metaphor, to take a specific example. Stars, beads, bones, heaven and earth, are all separated. And the string that joins them is obscure. It is Elizabeth Drury herself who is the "string" that yokes together "the most heterogeneous ideas" of heaven and earth. Elizabeth is the divine mediating metaphor that links with considerable difficulty the extremes of heaven and earth. It is her death that unlocks the door for all those who would follow her to heaven. Poet and reader alike must contemplate and celebrate her passing, imitating it in *mortem raptus* or ecstatic death. Wit's creation of Elizabeth as a divine metaphor is confirmed by the ecstasy which changes earthly perspective to a heavenly one. From that new vantage, fragmented earth is reorganized; nature has become transcendent through *discordia concors*, a yoking of opposites.

Having followed Elizabeth's soul to heaven, Donne understandably does not wish to fall back down to earth (*S.A.* 321-24):

> Returne not, my soule, from this extasee,
> And meditation of what thou shalt bee,
> To earthly thoughts, till it to thee appeare,
> With whom thy conversation must be there.

Having experienced such joy, he fears contamination with such earthly imperfection (*S.A.* 325-27):

> With whom wilt thou Converse? what station
> Canst thou choose out, free from infection
> That wil nor give thee theirs, nor drinke in thine?

To avoid the soul's descent from heavenly bliss, Donne tries to sustain his rapture (*S.A.* 339-40, 356-57):

> Up, up, my drowsie soule, where thy new eare
> Shall in the Angels songs no discord heare;
> * * *
> Up, up, for in that squadron there doth live
> Shee [Elizabeth].

John Donne: Yoking of Opposites

Forced to consider that one cannot spend his entire life in a rhapsodic state, Donne ponders Elizabeth's earthly life. Its perfection was such that she "could not fall / To worse, by company" (*S.A.* 376-77). If her virtues could be imitated, perhaps the poet's life would not be blemished. Donne meditates further on the meaning and implications of his rapture (*S.A.* 383-84):

> But pause, My soule, and study ere thou fall
> On accidentall joyes, th'essentiall.

The central question now becomes, quite simply, how does one live on earth cheerfully (*S.A.* 387-89):

> what essentiall joy canst thou effect
> Here upon earth? what permanent effect
> Of transitory causes?

Looking at man's "casuall happinesse" (*S.A.* 412)—so trivial, so flawed, and in its etymological sense, "fallen"—Donne concludes that "To erect true joye, were all the meanes in one" (*S.A.* 424), that is, to achieve true joy the means are all and only one: the "onely God, who ever must / Be sought alone" (*S.A.* 431-32). God is the only means of true happiness on earth. Thus, the poet attempts to work up to his "first pitch" (*S.A.* 435) again (*S.A.* 436-39):

> Know that all lines which circles doe containe,
> For once that they the center touch, do touch
> Twice the circumference; and be thou such.
> Double on Heaven, thy thoughts on Earth emploid.

If we can but find the center of God's circle on earth, our thoughts may "double on Heaven." True happiness may be regained, but (*S.A.* 440-44):

> All will not serve; Onely who have enjoyd
> The sight of God, in fulnesse, can thinke it;
> For it is both the object, and the wit.
> This is essentiall joye, where neither hee
> Can suffer Diminution, nor wee.

That only those who have seen God "can thinke it; / For it is both the object, and the wit" is an exceedingly condensed thought. The pronoun "it" ambiguously refers to two things at once. "It" is the "object" (that all good men seek) of seeing

John Donne: Yoking of Opposites

earth as an adumbration of heavenly harmony, in which all the fragmented "peeces" are tied together coherently, but "it" simultaneously is the "wit" or means of creating the ecstasy that ties all together and permits one to see the "object": "The sight of God." Living, Elizabeth had such "essentiall joye"; once we understand her, we have the "Idea" of "Woman" and its implications for mankind—from the Fall to our resurrection in Christ, the harmonizer.

Since Elizabeth "saw" God's circle everywhere on earth, poet and reader may achieve the same "object" by means of their "wit." For Donne, wit's method is *discordia concors*, and as divine metaphor, Elizabeth Drury personifies it. Her death has become the "patterne" "for life, and death" (*S. A.* 524), and the means of our doubling upon heaven, for the pattern is, of course, the circle that centers and ends in God. "By making full perfection grow," Elizabeth "Peeces a Circle" (*S.A.* 507-8). If we emulate her excellence, we may reunite heaven and earth.

Through *discordia concors*, a yoking of opposites, Donne's wit generated the divine metaphor of Elizabeth Drury, which permitted his soul to follow hers up to heaven. From the rapturous perspective of eternity, the poet understands that it is Christ who has reordered the fragmented world of *The First Anniversary*. It is the actual process of *discordia concors*—of wit's creation of divine metaphor—in *The Second Anniversary* that has reestablished God's "patterne" on earth, for all to read its lore.

When she was still alive, Elizabeth was so familiar "with God's presence" (*S.A.* 451, 452-54)

> as to know
> His face, in any naturall Stone, or Tree,
> Better then when in Images they bee.

Her perfection was such that she became a sacred book herself (*S.A.* 311-14):

> Shee, who in th'Art of knowing Heaven, was growen
> Here upon Earth, to such perfection,
> That shee hath, ever since to Heaven shee came,
> (In a far fairer print,) but read the same.

That mortals now on earth might experience the same "essentiall joye" which the "sight of God" brought Elizabeth, they must meditate on her example. She thus becomes the medium through which God is apprehended. The difficulties are great, but Elizabeth's is a model of goodness that all must aspire to, for after her death (*F.A.* 16-18),

> no other way there is
> But goodnes, to see her, whom all should see,
> All must endevour to be good as shee.

In other words, to be "in Heaven on Earth" one must do "Heavens workes" (*S.A.* 154). Through meditation on Elizabeth's goodness and through virtuous actions of their own, men may also come to reflect her pattern, which is also God's ("A Funerall Elegie" 97-104):

> if after her
> Any shall live, which dare true good prefer,
> Every such person is her delegate,
> T'accomplish that which should have beene her fate.
> They shall make up that booke, and shall have thankes
> Of fate and her, for filling up their blanks.
> For future vertuous deeds are Legacies,
> Which from the gift of her example rise.

The pages which Elizabeth did not fill, because of her own death, must be filled by those delegates who follow her path. She "cals us after her, in that shee tooke, / (Taking herselfe) our best, and worthiest booke" (*S.A.* 319-20). It is the "circle" of Elizabeth's perfection that one must see, judge, and follow. These are the proper callings of the soul. By reading in the volume that she epitomizes—now ecstatically transformed by divine metaphor—one's soul may, as Elizabeth's did, enjoy "the sight of God." Visible, physical, sensory data teach us that the world is a dead "carcasse," a burnt "cinder," "rubbidge," but wit aided by faith teaches the soul to "see, and Judge, and follow worthinesse, / And by Deedes praise it" (*F.A.* 4-5). By recognizing, judging, and following Elizabeth's worthy example, Donne revives not only Elizabeth but a dead world, and brings heaven and earth together again. Readers are implicitly invited to do likewise (*F.A.* 5-6):

John Donne: Yoking of Opposites

> He who doth not this,
> May lodge an In-mate soule, but tis not his.

Since Donne is primarily concerned with the construction of poetic arguments and metaphors that reflect the difficulty of yoking heterogeneous ideas, the actual poetic procedure of yoking contraries becomes the focal point of Donnean metaphysical wit "as a kind of *discordia concors*." Later in the century there is a decline in elaborately wrought, tortured arguments that attempt to resolve contrariety. The retreat from an ostensibly argumentative mode may moreover be equated with a growing inability to restore concord in the Donnean manner.

As Donnean violence subsides, to be replaced by a gentler, less eristic style and tone, verse becomes more allusive. Increasingly it is context rather than explicit logical structure that defines the terms being compared. Rather than set up such Donnean propositions as "Let mans Soule be a Spheare," subsequent poets refrain from a similarly abstract and geometric precision, preferring not to work within this kind of limitation. The multiplicity of meanings permitted by a more allusive language allows later metaphysical poets to deal with a discordant world in ways quite foreign to John Donne.

THREE

GEORGE HERBERT: DISCOVERY OF OCCULT RESEMBLANCES

Although related to the violent Donnean yoking of opposites, whose purpose is to transcend earthly contrariety, George Herbert's wit is informed by a *discordia concors* that depends less upon violence than upon the "discovery of occult resemblances in things apparently unlike." Such a revelation is a "discovery" or opening of that which is "occult" or concealed, rather than magical or Hermetic. Initially Herbert sets up an apparent dichotomy between two opposite complexities in *The Temple*: true ones, which God transforms and makes most plain, and false ones, produced by human artifice which the poet seems to equate with playing games. But finally the two are conflated as the falsity of human "invention" is purified and the secular comes to reflect the sacred in both art and life.

"The Sinner" illustrates the first kind of complexity, in which earthly contrariety is finally changed into its spiritual opposite by God. The poet sits down and writes about the miseries of his own life; his wit creates "earthly" metaphors, but they bring no ease. In despair he confesses:[1]

>   Lord, how I am all ague, when I seek
> What I have treasur'd in my memorie!

The treasured memory is of God's image which once dwelt within his heart until it turned to "quarries of pil'd vanities." The search for God's image within the heart's mine produces

> But shreds of holinesse, that dare not venture
> To shew their face, . . .
>
> * * *
>
> In so much dregs the quintessence is small.

Although he delves deep within his stony heart to find "heav'n the centre," he learns instead how vast "the circumference earth is." The sinner's predicament is such that the more he digs, the more he finds himself immersed in "earth," immured in a heart of stone, the soul enthralled to sin.

Unable to extract more than an infinitesimal amount of "quintessence" or gold, sinful man suddenly realizes the futility of striving to assure his own salvation, and so at last he surrenders to God's mercy:

> Yet Lord restore thine image, heare my call:
> And though my hard heart scarce to thee can grone,
> Remember that thou once didst write in stone.

Having described his spiritual condition as stony, the poet finally perceives that earthly metaphors do not solve the complexities and contrarieties of life. For his metaphors to work, God must transform them, and bring the poet the ease he cannot himself create.

Like Donne, who declares in the *Devotions* that God converts earthly "afflictions" into "remedies," Herbert sees that Scripture "makes good" ("The H. Scriptures II") his secular metaphor of the stony heart—for once, indeed, God did "write in stone" when he handed down the Ten Commandments to Moses, an event which moreover foreshadows the time when Christ's Passion would supplant the Old Testament laws with a new covenant of grace, "written not with ink, but with the Spirit of the living God; not in tables of stone, but in fleshy tables of the heart" (2 Cor. 3:3). The "discovery of occult resemblances" between the sinner's life and Scripture thus turns despair to hope; for the Lord's grace might still refine his "quarries of pil'd vanities" to "quintessence." Without God, man's heart is a mine whose stone can scarcely be pierced, but with God, man's redemption is assured: Mary's "holy mine" disclosed Christ the "gold," whose transforming grace is "The great restorative for all decay / In young and old" ("To all Angels and Saints" 11-13).

The sinner's despair is turned into hope not by the violent yoking of these opposites, which Donne assuredly would attempt, but by quietly dissolving the disparity that initially separates them. Resolution of the sinner's sense of exile from God is accomplished through that gentle, rather poignant, allusion to Scripture: "Remember that thou once didst write in stone." This single line converts sadness into gladness; it is neither further elaborated nor explained. Complicated, flamboyant, tortured Donnean arguments, combined with esoteric imagery, do not precede the allusion.[2] In fact, there is a striking absence of the distorted violence so characteristic of *The Second Anniversary*, in which Donne creates with exceeding difficulty the mediating metaphor of Elizabeth Drury, the string that yokes a distant heaven with earth. At the close of "The Sinner" we witness only the surrender of a frail spirit to God, for Herbert realizes that his metaphors neither solve nor mediate, nor bring ease until God perfects them. And yet the scriptural allusion was not casually introduced, nor seemingly tacked on inadvertently in the manner of Vaughan; it is carefully prepared for in the secular metaphor of the sinner's heart of stone.

The appropriateness of the biblical reference is based upon an associational linkage—like Donne's "afflictions" and "remedies" that, although spiritual opposites, are both "waters"—rather than an ostensibly logical progression. Herbert depicts his life in terms of a stony heart, and then suddenly God's holy "words do finde me out, & parallels bring, / And in another make me understood" ("H. Scriptures II"). The "discovery of occult resemblances" between the poet-sinner's life and Scripture resolves all "agues."[3] Truly Scripture does "make up some Christians destinie," for biblical figures and events are read into each man's life, just as in "The Sinner." And when God's metaphors "finde" him "out," the poet sees that where his own striving had discovered only "the circumference earth," "heav'n lies flat"—open—in the Bible ("H. Scriptures I"). Scripture easily restores "heav'n the centre" to the sinner, which ironically no amount of his own searching could reveal. By means of holy writ the secular metaphors of Herbert's wit have been converted into divine metaphors. Thus when man opens his heart to God, he learns that earthly discord may be banished and contrariety dissolved.

Throughout *The Temple* Herbertian wit frequently depends upon just such a strategy in which a melancholy, earth-and-time-bound state of mind is dramatically translated into its joyous opposite. Of course, not every poem makes such transformations, but then the resolution usually lies but a poem or two away, as does "To all Angels and Saints, " which "comments on" both "Avarice" and "The Sinner." To read *The Temple*, then, one must read it as Herbert does the Bible ("H. Scriptures II"):

> This verse marks that, and both do make a motion
> Unto a third, that ten leaves off doth lie.

More importantly, however, the solution and relief that God's scriptural metaphors bring to the complexities of the sinner's discordant life are based, as we can determine from the two "H. Scriptures" poems, upon the underlying assumption that biblical metaphor is not simply figuratively but literally true. Like Sir Thomas Browne, who came to perceive the truth of man as a microcosm—"I thought it onely a pleasant trope of Rhetorick, till my neare judgement and second thoughts told me there was a reall truth therein" (*R.M.* 1. 34)—we are also meant to interpret Herbert's metaphors as "reall." If, based upon their claim to fundamental truth, both *The Temple* and the Bible are viewed in the same parallel relationship, then Scripture can indeed, as Herbert asserts, "make up some Christians destinie" ("H. Scriptures II"). In the very act of writing about his life in verse, Scripture may transform both poem and life, and make them not only true but plain.

There is a second kind of complexity, however, that the

"Jordan" and the first two "Love" poems reveal as false invention and intricacy, which seeks not to disclose God's truth but to conceal it. The construction of riddling and obscure verse is an act of vanity that searches not for God, but dallies with human love. In "Love I" Herbert complains that "mortall love" has "parcel'd out" God's "glorious name" of "Immortall Love," "and thrown it on [the] dust." Worse, "mortall love" sides "with invention" or versifying, so that God, the proper object of poetry, is totally ignored. So engrossed are the lovers in composing amorous verse that instead of man's wit rising to praise the Creator, "Wit fancies beautie, beautie raiseth wit." Man's wit has looked on mortal beauty, a lovely lady, and *she*, not God, "raiseth" his "wit," enabling him to indite love lyrics to celebrate her glorious attributes. Herbert laments that "The world is theirs; they two play out the game, / Thou standing by." The "invention" and contrivance of false, mortal complexities is thus ostensibly equated with playing games. This is especially true since courtly (and later, Petrarchan) love emphasized the knight's devoted service to the lady, who was usually married to someone else. The love of the knight and lady was idealized. Since the woman was ultimately unattainable, the relationship was rather static; for although the man fervently pursued the woman, she remained equally constant to her honor, so that (with some famous exceptions as Tristan and Isolde, and Lancelot and Guinevere) such love is unfulfilled and unconsummated. In a real sense it was *jeux*—games to play, to feign, for the amusement and *jouissance* of a highly educated, sophisticated court society. In the act of playing their games the mortal lovers of "Love I" have all but forgotten God, the proper object of devotion. Dismayed, Herbert plaintively asks

> Who sings thy praise? onely a skarf or glove
> Doth warm our hands, and make them write of love.

The "skarf" and "glove" are the coveted tokens of a Petrarchan lover. It is a bitter statement that only they inspire the poet to write of a love aimed not at God, but the lady.

In "Love II" Herbert prays that God's "Immortall Heat"

will "kindle in our hearts such true desires, / As may consume our lusts":

> Then shall our hearts pant thee; then shall our brain
> All her invention on thine Altar lay,
> And there in hymnes send back thy fire again.

If God will but let his "greater flame / Attract the lesser to it" then the lust that leads mortal love to create false inventions shall be consumed and burnt away. Then "all wits shall rise, / And praise him who did make and mend our eies." But the word "consume" may also be taken in another sense. If God will but "assimilate" or "transform" mortal lusts into pure desires, then the possibility of true praise of the Creator's works is renewed. What Herbert seems to reject in the Petrarchan lovers is their taking God's "great frame" and "world" as their own, but "mortall love"—the "skarf" and "glove"—is but a portion of it. If God's "Immortall Heat" will "consume," that is, complete, perfect, and indeed, consummate the partial loves of courtly lovers, then shall God's greater "beautie" inspire "all wits" to "rise" and praise the Lord's creations in true "hymnes" and true "invention."

Another apparent rejection of false complexity occurs in "Jordan (I)" where Herbert is distressed at the dominance of false "invention."[4]

> Who sayes that fictions onely and false hair
> Become a verse? Is there in truth no beautie?
> Is all good structure in a winding stair?
> May no lines passe, except they do their dutie
>   Not to a true, but painted chair?
>
> Is it no verse, except enchanted groves
> And sudden arbours shadow course-spunne lines?
> Must purling streams refresh a lovers loves?
>   Catching the sense at two removes?

Herbert seems to reject "fictions" as "Catching the sense at two removes." The artificial, sugar-coated, highly ornate, mannered quality of so much courtly, "mortall" verse—the "false hair," the "enchanted groves" where Petrarchan lovers hide from one another and play their games—is a concealment of the true meaning. Since, moreover, Petrarchan love is perpetually unfulfilled, its dalliance requires continual diversion: "winding," "purling" (rippling rather than tranquil streams), "sudden arbours" for unexpected surprises, and "enchanted groves" for variety, mystery, and amusement. Similarly, the classical concept of poetry that presents universal truths through feigned examples is to be exchanged for telling truth directly. Rather than create verisimilitude in pleasing fictions, Herbert intends to portray man and the world as they really are. The verse of *The Temple* will reflect truth neither allegorically nor ideally, but as Scripture does.

The last stanza of "Jordan (I)" is important because it reveals not only how Herbert believed poetry ought to be composed, but also how it must be read:

> Shepherds are honest people; let them sing:
> Riddle who list, for me, and pull for Prime:
> I envie no mans nightingale or spring;
> Nor let them punish me with losse of rime,
>   Who plainly say, *My God, My King.*

The significance of this stanza is scarcely "plain" (from Latin *planus*, "flat") in the usual meaning of "open," "simple," or "without ambiguity." Herbert is punning, as he does throughout *The Temple*, on another sense of the word (from Latin *plenus*, "full"), to express the idea of "full, plenary, entire, perfect" (*OED*). The first line, then, "Shepherds are honest people; let them sing," is densely allusive. That "shepherds" is not limited or qualified in any manner, in itself becomes pertinent. As soon as one wonders *which* or *what kind of* shepherds are to sing, a multitude of possibilities crowds the stage for audition, and yet, from another point of view, all the possibilities are related. Since Christianity absorbed both the pagan tradition of the simple shepherd-poet in Arcady, and the Old Testament account of David, who composed and sang the Psalms in praise of God, the Gospels' presentation of Christ as shepherd, the pastor and feeder of his flocks, was typically interpreted as the fulfillment of all preceding shepherd-poets. Similarly, Christ's followers who later taught the Word are shepherds. Moreover, in real life Herbert was himself both poet and priest. Bemerton parishioners and readers of *The Temple* constitute his flock. Although differing in degree, each of these many shepherds is of kind the same. Those who foreshadow Christ, the shepherd, and those who imitate him in aftertimes, each "plainly" proclaims *one* thing—"*My God, My King*"—the single, obvious, and plain answer to all complexity and contrariety.

Fundamental to Herbert's verse, the paradox of speaking plainly accounts in part for the seeming simplicity of his highly sophisticated, complicated poetry. The poetic theory of hidden plainness is largely derived from the third and fourth chapters of Paul's second epistle to the Corinthians: "Seeing then that we have such hope [Christian mercy], we use great plainness of speech: And not as Moses, *which* put a vail over his face . . . which *vail* is done away in Christ." When that veil is removed, "we all, with open face beholding as in a glass the glory of the Lord, are changed into the same image from glory to glory." Strengthened by such knowledge,

we faint not; but have renounced the hidden things of dishonesty, not walking in craftiness, nor handling the word of God deceitfully; but by manifestation of the truth. . . . But if our gospel be hid, it is hid to them that are lost: in whom the god of this world hath blinded the minds of them which believe not, lest the light of the glorious gospel of Christ, who is the image of God, should shine unto them.

The Pauline principle of speaking with hidden plainness is thus directly related to the manifestation of God's truth, while the removal of the veil [recall in "Jordan (II)" the question, "Must all be vail'd?"] is implicitly linked with loving truth, a task eminently suited to "honest" shepherds. Yet the truth must always be hidden and veiled from those who would use "the word of God deceitfully." Consequently, Paul explains, "we speak the wisdom of God in a mystery, *even* the hidden *wisdom*, which God ordained before the world unto our glory. . . . But God hath revealed *them* [his secrets] unto us by his Spirit: for the Spirit searcheth all things, yea, the deep things of God" (1 Cor. 2:7, 10).

The lyrics in *The Temple* explore the kinds of complexities that are God's and those that are ostensibly only mortal. Many exemplify Herbert's "discovery" that however "occult" or hidden God's wisdom might be, the Lord himself is the single, "plain," and perfect answer. "Jordan (II)" itself re-presents and re-creates just such a discovery and comments upon it:

> When first my lines of heav'nly joyes made mention,
> Such was their lustre, they did so excell,
> That I sought out quaint words, and trim invention;
> My thoughts began to burnish, sprout, and swell,
> Curling with metaphors a plain intention,
> Decking the sense, as if it were to sell.

One is immediately reminded of the "invention" associated in "Love I" with human rather than heavenly love. The piling of one metaphor on another so entangles "a plain intention" that what was but playing an erotic game in "Love I" here becomes more ostensibly tainted. In the earlier "Love" poems flames of lust raised the wit of "mortall love," which Herbert now sadly discovers in his *own* verse. Like Marvell in "The Coronet" he perceives the flaw within his worthy impulse:

> As flames do work and winde, when they ascend,
> So did I weave my self into the sense.

As soon as soon as "self" complicates the "plain intention" of praising God, the poem becomes perverted. The self, Herbert believes, is never *the* answer; it is actually the complication that must be unwoven if "A Wreathed garland of deserved praise" ("A Wreath") is to be created and contrariety eased.

While seeking the quaint and remote term to deck and conceal the simple desire to praise the Lord, the poet suddenly hears "a friend / Whisper ["Jordan (II)"]:

> *How wide is all this long pretence!*
> *There is in love a sweetnesse readie penn'd:*
> *Copie out onely that, and save expense.*

In the Renaissance "onely" signified "one," as well as "only" in its modern sense. There is, of course, but one "love" to copy and that is God's. As the apostle Paul says, "We preach not ourselves, but Christ Jesus the Lord" (2 Cor. 4:5). The self ought not to be woven into the "sense," for it is God's. Again, by couching his "plain intention" in deliberately dense language, the poet is obliquely commenting upon the Pauline style of hidden plainness. Since "copie" means to imitate another's works, and since God is "authour of this great frame"—the Bible, the world, the poem, and *The Temple* itself—Herbert must seek heavenly inspiration so that his metaphors may be fulfilled and validated as divine. In rhetorical terminology, moreover, "copie" refers to the amplification of a topic—here, the relationship between man and his Creator. Although the lyrics frequently illustrate how difficult it is to realize "*There is in love a sweetnesse readie penn'd*," one learns that to "plainly say, *My God, My King*" actually requires a "plain," that is, "full" vocabulary—a *copia verborum*—filled not with "curling . . . metaphors," but with words that are open, yet hidden to those who would despise God's "workmanship" ("Love I").

To compose sacred verse, Herbert indicates he will "plainly say, *My God, My King*" neither by "riddl[ing]" nor by "pull[ing] for Prime." In "Jordan (I)" he appears to make a careful distinction between himself and other poets who "riddle" darkly just for the game of it. Herbert, on the other hand, through a pun on the word "prime," hints that his verse must be read as Scripture—as "reall" and true—not "at two removes." The complications of false wit and its inventions are "vail'd" simply to tease and puzzle the reader. If, however, *The Temple* is read directly, at *one* remove, the metaphors of sacred verse are taken in their "primary" or etymological sense. Consequently, all "tropes" become "reall," and all metaphors "plain." And since they are also "prime," or "one," they always read the same: "*My God, My King*."

In "Love I" Herbert deplored the amorous pair who "play out the game" and sing of their own love rather than praise God who dearly purchased their redemption. Analogously, in so far as it is a game, to "pull for Prime" is also rejected. Herbert's editor, the late F. E. Hutchinson, notes that the phrase is an allusion to the card game primero, but he does not completely explain its significance. I believe that the reference to primero is central to the poetic theories set forth in *The Temple* and to our understanding of Herbert's wit as the "discovery of occult resemblances in things apparently unlike."

Once exceedingly popular among the nobility, primero is a gambling card game that has now entirely disappeared, to the extent that few even recognize its name. A close modern counterpart is five-card draw poker. In primero four cards are dealt face-down to each player, who may at his discretion discard any or all of his cards in the hope of "pulling" a better card, and so "improve" his hand. Bets are then placed and the cards revealed. Of several desirable hands, one may win the "rest" (a sum of money agreed upon before bets are made) by "being prime," that is, by possessing one card of each suit.[5]

In "The Church-Porch" primero is again alluded to in the poet's advice to the reader to "Get a good stock of these [virtues], then draw the card / That suites him best, of whom thy speech is heard" (293-94). The wise man *shows* his best, "prime" qualities, "But a proud ignorance will lose his rest, / Rather then shew his cards" (297-98). The terms of primero thus begin to take on symbolic status in *The Temple*, for they illustrate the poet's moral belief that to "win" one's "rest"—that is, heavenly rest—one must simply "shew" one's hand and heart. A "proud ignorance" holds back, concealing his cards, thinking to do better by pulling another card. But pulling is equivalent to striving, and in *The Temple* striving always ironically leads to restlessness. Thus, in this interpretation, concealing one's hand is like riddling and veiling a "plain intention." And all are games that "mortall love" plays.

That the goal is rest is reiterated throughout the *The Temple*. "The Pulley" is, for instance, entirely built upon a conflict between heavenly "rest" and earthly "restlesnesse." Its wit centers in man's search for ease, which becomes the "pulley" that draws him up to God. Herbert imagines God's creation of man (3-5):

> Let us (said he) poure on him all we can:
> Let the worlds riches, which dispersed lie,
> Contract into a span.

As the heavenly virtues flow forth—"wisdome, honour, pleasure"—the Lord suddenly stops, "Perceiving that alone of all his treasure / Rest in the bottome lay" (9-10). "Rest" is the last "jewell" in the "glasse of blessings" and if it were also bestowed, man might "rest in Nature, not the God of Nature." To prevent such misplaced devotion, "rest" is apparently denied (16-20):

> Yet let him keep the rest [of the virtues],
> But keep them with repining restlesnesse:
> Let him be rich and wearie, that at least,
> If goodnesse leads him not, yet wearinesse
> May tosse him to my breast.

Frequently the poet himself does not recognize the "occult resemblances" between his life and holy doctrine, which answer man's weariness. "The Answer" displays Herbert as a failure in the eyes of the world:

> My comforts drop and melt away like snow:
> I shake my head, and all the thoughts and ends,
> Which my fierce youth did bandie, fall and flow
> Like leaves about me: or like summer friends,
> Flyes of estates and sunne-shine.

Once possessed of great expectations at court, young Herbert upon the death of his patrons was reduced to taking a small parish living. Compared to the "thoughts and ends" which his "fierce youth did bandie," his later life as country parson appears ruined—a provincial bore. Replying to all those "Who think me eager, hot, and undertaking, / But in my prosecutions slack and small," the poet compares his loss of fame and advancement to a cycle of weather. Former aspirations are "As a young exhalation, newly waking, / Scorns his first bed of dirt, and means the sky." A vapor, or young, spirited, ambitious man, of course, tends to rise to the sky,

> But cooling by the way, grows pursie and slow,
> And setling to a cloud, doth live and die
> In that dark state of tears.

But, like tears, rain is an integral part of earthly life and cannot be avoided. The sun, however, eventually evaporates and draws the rain up to the sky. Although this final stage of the cycle is not overtly mentioned, implicitly it is the warming work of the sun (Son), Jesus Christ, who will lift the faithful soul to its heavenly rest. Herbert thus describes his own condition in earthly metaphor, and scriptural metaphor answers it, assuring him that "rest" is his effortlessly, not by scorning the "first bed of dirt," by actively striving or pulling for success, but by accepting the "dark state of tears," until the Son pulls the soul up to rest in heaven (cf. "The Pulley"). To understand that one is saved not by his own efforts, but by God's providential mercy, is always the answer in *The Temple*. "The Answer" is thus representative of a process of discovery. "Occult resemblances" "finde" the poet out and uncover a pattern which reassures him that heavenly rest is his eventually. In "A True Hymne" Herbert cries out, "O, could I love!" and "God writeth 'Loved.' " When the poet attempts to solve dilemmas himself in "much wrastling" and "many a combate" ("The Crosse" 8), then "contrarieties crush" him and "winde a rope about, and cut [his] heart" (32-33). But emotional conflict is eased by Christ, as Herbert realizes in the last lines (34-36):

> And yet since these thy contradictions
> Are properly a crosse felt by thy Sonne,
> With but foure words, my words, *Thy will be done*.

Having discovered "occult resemblances" between his own suffering and Christ's Passion, Herbert sees himself as a cross, but only Christ's solves the contradictions of daily life.

The answer to contrariety in Herbert's verse invariably consists of surrender to God. That ability depends upon Christ's validating the poet's secular metaphors and assuring him that they are indeed divine rather than false complexities sprung from a false wit. In contrast to Donne's strategy of initially separating as far as possible what appear as contraries, and then constructing a quasi-logical argument that will violently yoke them through an arduously constructed mediating metaphor, Herbert simply describes his own life, which seems blocked by contrary emotions; but instead of yoking such opposites, he discovers that they are relieved by Christ in scriptural metaphor. By his discovering an answer in God, discord is dissolved rather than forcefully yoked. Thus, Donne's poems typically close violently—whether he has successfully joined opposites or failed—while Herbert's typically close in contented ease after "much wrestling" and "many a combate." Herbertian wit is characterized by the realization that only God can make everything "fit" harmoniously; and only God can mend the defects and discords of art and human nature. When compared to Scripture, the contraries in Herbert's life find their complement. The resulting pattern assuages the agony that discord brings.

In "The Forerunners" we find the poet much older, wondering aloud if, in advancing age, he shall be able to write: "Farewell sweet phrases, lovely metaphors. / But will ye leave me thus?" (13-14). But even should the lovely, purified metaphors depart, the poet can yet fervently assert: "*Thou art still my God*" (32) which is, in fact, all that mellifluous phrases "Perhaps with more embellishment can say" (33). The "sparkling notions" (4) of youth shall disappear, but it matters little, for decorative language can say no more than "*Thou art still my God*," the only true rest. "The Forerunners" thus reaches the same paradoxical conclusion as the "Jordan" poems. Like the "plainly" said "*My God, My King*," Christ's doctrine ("Divinitie" 14) "Was cleare as heav'n, from whence it came" (21-24):

> But he [Christ] doth bid us take his bloud for wine.
>   Bid what he please; yet I am sure,
> To take and taste what he doth there designe,
>   Is all that saves, and not obscure.

To rest in Christ is "not obscure" doctrine, but the poet repeatedly demonstrates throughout *The Temple* how difficult it is to discover and "shew" such an apparently simple solution to contrariety and false complexity.

In "Confession" "occult resemblances" must be read "for Prime"—not "at two removes" (1-6):

> O What a cunning guest
> Is this same grief! within my heart I made
> Closets; and in them many a chest;
> And, like a master in my trade,
> In those chests, boxes; in each box, a till:
> Yet grief knows all, and enters when he will.

Paradoxically, "Onely an open breast / Doth shut [God's afflictions] out, so that they cannot enter" (19-20).

The doctrine of the open heart may be likened to the poetic theories expressed in "Jordan (I)," in which "fictions," "false hair," "riddl[ing]," and "pull[ing] for Prime" are ostensibly rejected in favor of direct truth ("Confession" 23-24):

> Smooth open hearts no fastning have; but fiction
> Doth give a hold and handle to affliction.

Truth and rest exists in "open hearts" that show their concealed cards (25-30):

> Wherefore my faults and sinnes,
> Lord, I acknowledge; take thy plagues away:
> For since confession pardon winnes,
> I challenge here the brightest day,
> The clearest diamond: let them do their best,
> They shall be thick and cloudie to my breast.

One must simply lay down one's hidden cards to win the rest. The confession or disclosure of sins is the discovery, opening of one's closed heart, that "pardon winnes." When Scripture "finde[s]" the poet "out, & parallels bring," God's heavenly "secrets" lie revealed as much as man's faults do. But the disclosure confirms the answer that only Christ's Passion "winnes" both "pardon" and "rest" ("The Bag" 23-24):

> And having giv'n the rest before,
> Here he gave up his life to pay our score.

To gain rest, man must only confess or demonstrate his dependence upon Christ.

"Love (III)," the last poem in *The Temple*, most explicitly conflates the apparent dichotomies set forth earlier, for this poem perfects the false "invention" of mortal, Petrarchan lovers, whose scarf and glove represented praise for a small portion of God's creation, which they took for the entire world. Indeed, their fault is not so much that they love, but that their ardor is self-contained and never ascends to praise God, the Creator of all. In "Love (III)," however, the secular love ostensibly rejected in the "Jordan" and the first two "Love" poems is finally "consumed."

In "Love (III)" God appears to the poet as his beloved. Significantly, the language of the poem is that of sensuous, rather than Petrarchan love, for at last love is fulfilled: "You must sit down, sayes Love, and taste my meat" (17). At first the poet objects, feeling unworthy and guilty with sin, but Love assures him that he need not shrink back in fear, for God has already borne the blame of man's sins; salvation is already granted. The role of man and poet is simply to serve his beloved, as Love has already served him to win his rest.

Now at ease the poet receives his "guest," the Lord of Hosts, into the temple of his open heart. Guest and host, lover and beloved, merge and become indistinguishable from one another. Within the heart's temple Herbert tastes the "mysticall repast" ("Superliminare" 4) of the Holy Eucharist that represents Christ's body. The false complexities and games produced by human artifice that sought to riddle and conceal God's truth in the earlier poems are now "consumed"—not simply destroyed but actually eaten and assimilated. Taking the Lord into one's heart "consumes," in the sense of "consummates" or "completes," the imperfect and impartial inventions of secular poetry, created by the scarf and glove of mortal love. At last all wits may "rise" and truly praise the "Immortall Love, authour of this great frame" ("Love I"). Thus, the initial divisions are now entirely broken down and conflated by Herbert's use of *discordia concors*, which joins opposites, not violently but gently, through the "discovery of occult resemblances in things apparently unlike."

The final poem in *The Temple*, "Love (III)," now clarifies the first, "The Altar":

> A broken ALTAR, Lord, thy servant reares,
> Made of a heart, and cemented with teares:
>   Whose parts are as thy hand did frame;
>   No workmans tool hath touch'd the same.
>   A HEART alone
>   Is such a stone,
>   As nothing but
>   Thy pow'r doth cut.
>   Wherefore each part
>   Of my hard heart
>   Meets in this frame,
>   To praise thy Name.

His lusts consumed, the sinner may now hope to place "all [his] invention on thine Altar" ("Love II"). By serving God, the sinner's hard heart "Meets in this frame / To praise" the Lord of Love ("The Altar" 10, 11-12). The conflation of apparent opposites—secular and sacred verse and love—within "Love (III)" permits us to see that in the very first poem all was implicitly transformed by God. Within the circle of *The Temple*, however, Herbert learns and teaches the difficult lesson that God "finde [s]" man "out" in Scripture and in life. If the heart is open to "immortall Love," rest is assured. This knowledge permits the poet-sinner to "frame" his "invention" in imitation of the first author, God, who created all and is most worthy of praise.

Since Herbert uses *discordia concors* in dense, complex, and allusive language, rather than a more Donnean, strained and tortured argument, to yoke "the most heterogeneous ideas" together, it suggests that Herbert's verse is transitional between Donne and the later metaphysical poets. The comparatively gentle, intimately poignant tone of *The Temple*, with its metaphors that refer to several meanings at once, anticipates Marvell's highly sophisticated wit. At the same time Herbert shares many of the same thematic and stylistic concerns as Vaughan, who readily admitted the influence of *The Temple* upon *Silex Scintillans*. I believe, however, that the connection is even greater than Vaughan's borrowing of Herbert's imagery, and this suggests that Vaughan owes much to

Herbert's preoccupation with such paradoxical oppositions as the inner and outer, rest and unrest, open and closed, plain and occult, life and Scripture, ease and difficulty, and the figurative and true. But as it will be observed in the next chapter, Vaughan pushes Herbert's system much further and makes it a vehicle for the remarkable creation of paradoxes that reflect a state of regeneration.

FOUR

HENRY VAUGHAN: PARADOXES OF REGENERATION

The prevailing critical view that Henry Vaughan's poetry is "less vigorous, less ratiocinative, less torn, more nostalgic, credulous, and otherworldly" than John Donne's,[1] distorts our appreciation of Vaughan's wit. If Donne is most typically associated with the metaphysical style, then any variation from the Donnean manner suffers proportionately. A more careful reading of both poets, however, dispels the implicit disparagement of Vaughan who, although perhaps a poet of lesser stature, simply displays a style that diverges in many respects from Donne's.

Although exhibiting a variation of the Donnean yoking of opposites, whose purpose is transcendent, the wit of *Silex Scintillans* differs markedly from that in Donne's *Divine Poems* and *Anniversaries*. Donne frequently extends his metaphors from one image to another by a process of association, but he carefully marks the linkage in a seemingly logical progression. The combinations of metaphors and arguments may not withstand rigorous inspection, but initially the effect is persuasively "ratiocinative." When Donne declares, for example, "Let mans Soule be a Spheare," he is overtly connecting the tenor ("soule") of a metaphor with its vehicle ("spheare"), but Vaughan, on the contrary, may not *ever* mention the tenor. Without Donne's careful, even tortured creation of mediating metaphors that yoke opposites, Vaughan casually drops disconnected metaphors helter-skelter into poems as if by accident, capriciousness, or worse, inattention to craft. The apparently whimsical introduction of so much extraneous imagery is not only daring, it is startling and perplexing. And occasionally rather amusing as well. In "Sure, there's a tye of Bodyes!"[2] a poem about death and those who survive, Vaughan, for instance, boldly asserts that "man is such a Marygold," but the marigold metaphor did not *grow* out of any previously introduced imagery; Vaughan has simply injected it. Moreover, in one poem a metaphor may be understood in one manner, but in another poem the same metaphor may suggest a radically different interpretation.

When images and metaphors, such as herbs and flowers, are repeated extensively throughout *Silex Scintillans*, the repetition not only becomes confusing but it becomes sufficiently significant to suggest a conscious, rationally motivated poetic technique. In *Of Paradise and Light* E. C. Pettet rightly calls attention to "recurrent image-clusters," but he primarily attributes their recurrence to subconscious "associational linkage" on Vaughan's part.[3] Other theories attempt to unravel Vaughan's mysterious habit of inserting seemingly irrelevant metaphors, but none explains it adequately. Biographical sources are meager: Vaughan's interest in the arcane activities of his brother Thomas have suggested that the poetry is odd because Vaughan was a Hermetic philosopher or a mystic, but this explanation is finally useless because *every* inexplicable metaphor or dazzling paradox can then be attributed to a mystical experience. Moreover, mysticism, Hermeticism, and religious conversions from sin to piety, are difficult to prove and actually tend to avoid explication of the poetry.[4] It therefore seems better to account for Vaughan's bizarre style by dealing with it directly in the poetic text itself.

Recurrent image clusters do indeed unify *Silex Scintillans*, as Pettet concludes, but this important observation is potentially more illuminating than Pettet himself realizes.[5] Although imagery is always to some extent inspirational, I believe that the persistent echo and repetition of metaphor in *Silex Scintillans* is primarily a conscious symbolic technique. At some point Vaughan must have recognized that recurring images composed a pattern of contrariety which exactly corresponded to his deeply held beliefs about man, nature, and salvation. That pattern itself comprehends Vaughan's highly distinctive use of *discordia concors*.

Once *discordia concors* is revealed in *Silex Scintillans*, it does much to restore the conviction that Vaughan's poetry is "ratiocinative" and worthwhile in its own right, for previously it has been explained only by recourse to such terms as "subconscious association," "mystic," "occult," and Hermetic." *Discordia concors* is attractive precisely because it is so cogent, deliberate, and conscious. It can account for the recurring images and sudden paradoxes of Vaughan's distinctive style without our resorting to intrinsically irrational or supernatural explanations, all of which are external to the poetry itself. At the same time *discordia concors* exactly mirrors the philosophical and religious ideals set forth in the lyrics. Style and meaning are mutually interlocking in *Silex Scintillans*, and *discordia concors* provides the key to both.

Seeing the sun at midnight is the central paradox of Vaughan's great poem,[6] "The Night" (5-12):

> Wise *Nicodemus* saw such light
> As made him know his God by night.
>
> Most blest believer he!
> Who in that land of darkness and blinde eyes
> Thy long expected healing wings could see,
> When thou didst rise,
> And what can never more be done,
> Did at mid-night speak with the Sun!

Initially Scripture and mystic tradition appear to account for the appropriateness of this paradox. During their nocturnal encounter Christ reveals to Nicodemus (John 3:2) that a man must be reborn to see the kingdom of heaven. But how an old man might be reborn puzzles Nicodemus. The old man is of course the old Adam or original sin that all men possess since the Fall, but it is always possible for the old Adam to be regenerated. Those may be saved who see the light of the sun, Jesus Christ. Here light has the force of moral goodness, while darkness is linked with ignorance, evil, and the devil. Dark and light have always waged incessant war for the possession of man's soul. It is therefore surprising that Vaughan boldly proclaims that the nighttime, the usually evil hours of the Prince of Darkness, is the proper time to commune with Christ. To make this reversal in the moral value of night more explicit, Vaughan compresses all the wisdom of Nicodemus into the paradox of the wise man who "Did at midnight speak with the Sun!" The scriptural version does not reverse the traditional moral values that light and darkness possess. Nor does the biblical episode of Nicodemus begin to explain why, or how, Vaughan emphasizes night as the opposite of day, nor why, through a pun on Christ as "sun" and "Son," he has linked the nighttime with Christ.

There is, however, the entirely traditional paradox of the dark night of the soul, in which the customary attributes of night and day are reversed. The sixteenth-century Spanish mystic St. John of the Cross, for example, rejoices that "in this happy night of contemplation God leads the soul."[7] Surely the mystical dark night of the soul stimulated Vaughan's poetic imagination, but in "The Night" he has fused and augmented scriptural plot and mystic paradox to create a more forcefully symbolic statement (25-30):

> Dear night! this worlds defeat;
> The stop to busie fools; cares check and curb;
> The day of Spirits; my souls calm retreat
>   Which none disturb!
> *Christs* progress, and his prayer time;
> The hours to which high Heaven doth chime.

In "The Night" "*trees* and *herbs* did watch and peep / And wonder, while the *Jews* did sleep" (23-24). In this context the Jews are unregenerate; they should be up, awake with Nicodemus at the "dead and silent hour" (14) of midnight to talk with God. Since the poem is set in the "worlds ill-guiding light" (47), the night is the time to be alert if one is among the regenerate. Night thus corresponds to "the day of Spirits" and

"The hours to which high Heaven doth chime." Vaughan's strategy of creating contrariety by reversing the expected order of things is far more than simply an allusion to Scripture or mystic tradition; it is the structural plan not only of "The Night" but ultimately of *Silex Scintillans* itself, and it is Vaughan's own special use of *discordia concors*.

That Vaughan knew perfectly well what he was doing when he reversed the values of night and day may be determined through comparison with related poems in the *Silex* series. As an allegorical journey through life to salvation, "Regeneration" comments obliquely upon "The Night." The pattern outlined in the journey from illusion to true vision is mirrored in the changing value of the word "spring." While still enthralled to sin, the pilgrim escapes, stealing abroad into the world outdoors where "it was high-spring" (3), but his regeneration proves false: "sinne / Like Clouds ecclips'd my mind" (7-8). But having "perceiv'd my spring / Meere stage, and show" (9-10), he repents of his vanity. God's mercy then renews the possibility of salvation. Beckoned to the holy place where Jacob watched angels ascending and descending upon a ladder that stretched from earth to heaven, a vision of a "new spring" (39) is revealed to the penitent, wherein (41-43)

> The unthrift Sunne shot vitall gold
> A thousand peeces,
> And heaven its azure did unfold.

"Regeneration" thus progresses from the sham "high-spring" of false rebirth to its contrary, the spiritual "new spring" of true regeneration. "Spring" is Janus-like—symbolic of one thing and its opposite—of discord in a seeming concord.

The stones and flowers in the "new spring" of "Regeneration" are complex metaphors as well. In the cistern are stones —"some bright, and round / Others ill-shap'd, and dull" (55-56). The bright stones "as quick as light / Danc'd through the floud" (57-58), while the dull "more heavy then the night / Nail'd to the Center stood" (59-60). The flowers, too, are either "fast asleepe" or "broad-eyed / And taking in the Ray" (67-68). Read in isolation these passages present no difficulties in explication. R. A. Durr, for example, proposes that the stones "quick as light" and the flowers "broad-eyed / And taking in the Ray" during daytime are like those souls regenerated by Christ, the Son (sun), and therefore preferable to those "ill-shap'd, and dull," and "fast asleepe."[8] Alternate interpretations are possible, however. The stones "nail'd to the Center" might as easily refer to Christ's Crucifixion at the center of the world, thus implying regeneration. But comparison with related poems complicates the matter further. In "Silence, and stealth of dayes!" the center is obviously associated with goodness (29-32):

> Yet I have one *Pearle* by whose light
>   All things I see,
> And in the heart of Earth, and night
>   Find Heaven, and thee.

And if one recalls "The Night" in which "*trees* and *herbs* did watch and peep / And wonder, while the *Jews* did sleep," the wakeful plants were linked with Nicodemus who wisely sought the sun (Christ) at the midnight hour. At night sleeping corresponded to false regeneration, while watching suggested true rebirth. It is thus no longer a simple matter to evaluate the stones and flowers of "Regeneration." The contradictory testimony of repeated images, such as flowers, stones, sleeping and waking, is initially disconcerting, but an underlying stratagem does control the metaphors of *Silex Scintillans*, and it does not originate in the poet's or mystic's whimsical predilection for "diverse, and even conflicting, images of heaven."[9]

To understand the reversals in "The Night" and other poems, it is necessary to uncover and characterize the structural pattern governing the whole of *Silex Scintillans*. "Religion" summons up remembrance of that unfallen, gracious world, when angels conversed with man and the spirit of God permeated every wood and leaf and bower. But after man's sin/ communication faltered until at last "no Conf'rence" existed "in these daies" (20). "Is the truce broke?" (21) cries the poet; must miracles now cease? The answer reveals Vaughan's larger pattern of contrariety (29-35):

Henry Vaughan: Paradoxes of Regeneration

> No, no; Religion is a Spring
> That from some secret, golden Mine
> Derives her birth, and thence doth bring
> Cordials in every drop, and Wine;
>
> But in her long, and hidden Course
> Passing through the Earths darke veines,
> Growes still from better unto worse.

Although superficially "poison'd" (41), religion remains pure and uncorrupt deep within the earth's center. What was intended as "phisick" (44) may destroy. The "spring" of religion is thus both good and bad at once. In its "heart" it is a "cordial," the healing "wine" of Christ's own blood, but at its extremities it is "puddle, or meere slime" (43). To tap the pure spring of true religion, one must journey far, not in vain rovings throughout the natural world, but deep within the "groves" of scriptural "leaves" or pages, where God's "spirit doth still fan" (1-4):

> My God, when I walke in those groves,
> And leaves thy spirit doth still fan,
> I see in each shade that there growes
> An Angell talking with a man.

To find that spirit, one must look inside oneself in deep meditation. To respond only to the outward ceremonial trappings of the church is to be duped at once by "Meere stage, and show." Looking outward at appearances only is a vain and corrupt activity, while looking inward to the center is good. From "Regeneration" and "Religion" a significant pattern begins to emerge: reality is repeatedly associated with the inner, the spiritual, the heavenly, the regenerate, and the good, while appearance is associated with opposite qualities: the outer, the bodily, the earthly, the unregenerate, and the evil. This pattern illuminates "Sure, there's a tye of Bodyes!" "The Night," and ultimately, the whole of *Silex Scintillans*.

In the first stanza of "Sure, there's a tye of Bodyes!" man is very much moribund (3-4):

> Love languisheth, and memory doth rust
> O'r-cast with that cold dust.

As memory of departed loved ones fades and they "dissolve . . . to Clay" (2) and "cold dust," the "tye of Bodyes" that once joined men also seems to disappear (5-6):

> For things thus *Center'd*, without *Beames*, or *Action*
> Nor give, nor take *Contaction*.

In other words, in the world of appearance man seems "*center'd*" in despair, inactivity, and mourning. Having lost his "tye" or physical contact with the dead, the poet is centered in the continual process of decay without hope of regeneration. Left with a legacy of "cold dust," "man is such a Marygold" that, "these fled," he "shuts, and hangs the head" (7-8). Initially Vaughan's tone is derisive; with loved ones "fled," man "hangs the head" in a posture of despair, looking downwards toward the center, the grave, for he has so little faith in the invisible realm of spirit.

In stanza 1 man as marigold therefore suggests an unregenerate state, analogous to his immersion in the earthly in the poem "Corruption": "Sin triumphs still, and man is sunk below / The Center" (35-36). In "Religion" and "Silence, and stealth of dayes!" however, the center is clearly linked with heaven and purity, thus hinting that to be regenerate in the external world of appearance, man must do the opposite of the expected worldly gesture: he must, for instance, "hang the head" downwards toward the center, in order to "take *Contaction*" with dead loved ones. It is "souls must / Track one the other"; "the spirit, not the dust / Must be thy brother" ("Silence, and stealth of dayes!" 25-28).

The survivors lack the faith to perceive that the dead, who appear "invisible and dim," are not truly lost forever. The very image of the marigold's drooping head in the first stanza mirrors futility and pessimism, but in the second stanza of "Sure, there's a tye of Bodyes!" the very opposite occurs (11-12):

> Herbs sleep unto the *East*, and some fowles thence
> Watch the Returns of light.

Anticipating Christ, the rising sun, herbs and fowls are not deceived by false appearances as the marigold seems to have been in stanza 1. It must, however, be recognized that the first stanza is set within the context of the world of appearance, while the second represents the poet's world of spirit. If the marigold were in the second stanza, it too would "Watch the Returns of light" with head held high.

In external nature men are wrapped "in Imaginary flights / Wide of a faithfull grave" (15-16), where "false, short delights / Tell us the world is brave" (13-14). "False, short delights" unwittingly do tell us the truth—the world *is* "Meere stage, and show." Moreover, worldly superficiality is not only "short," but it prevents one from enjoying a "faithfull grave." Lazarus is vainly carried out of town physically to separate men from the actual embodiment of their fear of death. Vaughan, on the contrary, wishes to rejoin the dead (21-24):

> But I will be my own *Deaths-head*; and though
>   The flatt'rer say, *I live*,
> Because Incertainties we cannot know
>   Be sure, not to believe.

To reestablish contact with the dead, the poet must himself die before his natural death by turning inward to contemplate the grave, the gate through which the new light will come. In Vaughan's system the proper pose in a world of false appearances is the opposite of flatterers and fools. It is therefore appropriate that man the marigold shuts and hangs his head. By turning away from the "false, short delights" of the "brave," showy world, "Absents within the Line Conspire, and *Sense* / Things distant doth unite" (9-10). Whatever was separated by death is reunited. "Absents" do "conspire" in the etymological sense that they revive and "breath together" again. Sure, there *is* a tie of bodies, but it is "the spirit, not the dust / Must be thy brother."

Another of the untitled poems on the death of Vaughan's brother, "Thou that know'st for whom I mourne," reveals that vitality in the regenerate soul appears as death to the "Common Eye" of mortality (29-32):

> Thus hast thou plac'd in mans outside
>   Death to the Common Eye,
> That heaven within him might abide,
>   And close eternitie.

Henry Vaughan: Paradoxes of Regeneration

To the "Common Eye" of the "flatt'rer" in "Sure, there's a tye of Bodyes!" the regenerate man seems dead, but actually his life is within, where he communes with heaven ("The Incarnation, and Passion" 9-12):

> Brave wormes, and Earth! that thus could have
> A God Enclos'd within your Cell,
> Your maker pent up in a grave,
> Life lockt in death, heav'n in a shell.

To live, regenerate souls must *appear* dead to the "Common Eye" of the external world. The poet therefore prays, "*Let me dye before my death*" ("Regeneration" 82), so he may find heaven and eternity, the rightful end of all human activity.

The same pattern of contrariety created through reversals is repeated in "Come, come, what doe I here? / Since he is gone." The tomb appears "a dark, and seal'd up wombe, / Which ne'r breeds more" (23-24), but the poet implies that life may still emerge (27-30):

> But I would be
> With him I weep
> A bed, and sleep
> To wake in thee.

Metaphors of the bed and grave (including other related symbols) are so frequently repeated in the context of external nature that they become symbolic of regeneration, especially when associated with the world of night ("Joy of my life!" 9-10):

> Stars are of mighty use: The night
> Is dark, and long.

But "Gods Saints are shining lights" (17) that (21-24)

> all night
> Like Candles, shed
> Their beams, and light
> Us into Bed.

These symbols converge in "The Morning-watch." All the important reversals of customary worldly activity are here (23-33):

> O let me climbe
> When I lye down! The Pious soul by night
> Is like a clouded starre, whose beames though sed
>   To shed their light
>   Under some Cloud
>   Yet are above,
>   And shine, and move
> Beyond that mistie shrowd.
>   So in my Bed
> That Curtain'd grave, though sleep, like ashes, hide
> My lamp, and life, both shall in thee abide.

Although clouded and obscured to the "Common Eye," the "Pious soul" shines at night with an inner light. Through a series of imaginative parallels, the soul is linked with the star, the bed, and the grave, while the cloud is joined with the curtain and the misty shroud. The cloud surrounding the star parallels the curtain about the bed, which in turn corresponds to the misty shroud covering the body, and finally to the "ashes" that hide "my lamp, and life." To the world of appearance all seems dark, curtained, misty, and dead, but to the elect the soul's fire burns inwardly with a living flame.

In the context of the flatterer's world, the soul must lie down in the bed-grave to "climbe" to "heav'ns blisse" (22). This reversal is necessary because only action contrary to custom is evidence of election. Indeed, in Vaughan's representation of the regenerate soul, one appears to sleep in order to be the more awake. Most appropriately then, at night the "soul breakes, and buds" like a flower with "shoots of glory" ("Morning-watch" 2).

The flower metaphor reappears in "I Walkt the other day (to spend my hour,)," where again it is associated with metaphors of the grave, bed, and shroud.[10] The poet has strolled outdoors to spend his usual hour of meditation. It is wintertime and vegetation is sparse, ostensibly chilled to death by frost. Remembering where "a gallant flowre" (4) once had grown, Vaughan digs about and discovers its "other bowre" (14) or home for hibernation (18-21):

>   And by and by
> I saw the warm Recluse alone to lie
>   Where fresh and green
> He lived of us unseen.

Like "cold friends" (12), the flower is not really dead, but thriving beneath the surface. What seemed dead is simply recluse—shut away from winter and the gadding world of vanity. Since it is a substantive etymologically derived from the Latin *recludere* meaning both to open and to close, "recluse" is especially apposite. To the world of appearance the flower, like departed "cold friends," seems closed up in death, but to the world of spirit the flower opens "fresh and green" in "some other bowre." The poet thus regains hope that green life may still be hidden within his brother's tomb or bower (61-63):

> shew me his life again
> At whose dumbe urn
> Thus all the year I mourn.

Discovery of inner liveliness poignantly demonstrates to Vaughan how easily the "Masques and shadows" (50) of external nature are mistaken for reality.

If Vaughan accepted the Book of Nature as a valid means of discovering God, he certainly read it in a highly unconventional manner;[11] for nature is filled not with imperfect images that foreshadow heaven but with images that are vain, empty, and deceptive. And far from deifying nature, Vaughan ultimately transcends the physical, visible world to reach heaven through a yoking of opposites. Metaphors that transcend earth are necessarily taken from visible nature, simply because no other expressions are available. But Vaughan so repeatedly uses nature imagery that he has been mistaken for a "nature poet" and precursor of the romantics. We have already seen, however, that the values of the external world—the "high-spring"—are not as they first appear, synonymous with the good. Instead, the good belongs to the inner, invisible sphere of spirit, the "new spring" of heaven. "The Water-fall" follows such a pattern; at first the poet delights in visible nature as a great good: "Dear stream! dear bank, where often I / Have sate" (13-14). The final lines, however, abruptly shift from the actual waterfall to a spiritual one (37-40):

Henry Vaughan: Paradoxes of Regeneration

> O my invisible estate,
> My glorious liberty, still late!
> Thou [Christ] art the Channel my soul seeks,
> Not this with Cataracts and Creeks.

The natural waterfall is abandoned for Christ, the "channel." Thus, although external nature supplies metaphors to reach the infinite and invisible, it is ultimately rejected.

When nature failed for Vaughan, the way to heaven must have seemed barred. If heaven and earth are antithetical states, the poet requires some means to rejoin the spiritual with the mundane. For Vaughan the medium is *discordia concors*, but his distinctive use of the concept as a stylistic and metaphysical strategy is far more complicated than a simple Donnean yoking of opposites. Vaughan's first step is to discover the discord in a too easy concord. By turning away from the false, vain world of nature, he finds a truer one within the self ("Content" 21-24):

> Some Love a *Rose*
> In hand, some in the skin;
> But crosse to those,
> I would have mine *within*.

Although, strictly speaking, Vaughan's metaphors are not puns, they acquire this quality when contrasted in thematically related lyrics. At once they reflect two contrary states: the outside or "skin" is false and degenerate, while the inside is true and regenerate. Heaven is discovered by splitting a metaphor apart to reveal its inner and spiritual meaning ("Silence, and stealth of dayes!" 25-32):

> but the souls must
> Track one the other,
> And now the spirit, not the dust
> Must be thy brother.
> Yet I have one *Pearle* by whose light
> All things I see,
> And in the heart of Earth, and night
> Find Heaven, and thee.

Souls "track" one another by detecting the ambivalence within metaphors. The "heart of Earth, and night" are analogues of the human spirit and, as such, oppose the ephemeral world of mortal body and dust. Vaughan's earnest emphasis on the inner, the private, and the spiritual, is not necessarily Hermetic or mystical, but its private quality does suggest that his poetry is accessible only to readers willing to trace the spirit.

One of the greatest clues to Vaughan's use of *discordia concors* is the recognition that if one applies the usual moral distinctions to the world of appearances, one is always mistaken. If, for example, it is assumed that mourning and inactivity in "Sure, there's a tye of Bodyes!" is a sign of degeneration, then one has mistaken the elect for the damned. The world of nature actually idolizes or parodies the world of spirit. Appearance ironically seems *identical* with the spiritual, but in fact "*The world did only paint and lie*"["Mount of Olives" (II) 10] and is the spirit's very opposite.

With rarely appreciated genius, Vaughan has detected the masquerade of sin as salvation. Throughout *Silex Scintillans* he enlarges this basic insight to imply that what seems concord to the "Common Eye," such as the "high-spring," is actually discord. In Vaughan's new development of *discordia concors*, paradoxically the process toward truth is initially one of division. Knowing that the eye is enticed by the "Meere stage, and show" of the "high-spring," he deliberately permits us to be ensnared by a false vision of regeneration. The parodic goodness of the "high-spring" has to be split apart to reveal its opposite, the "new spring" of heaven. The Janus-face of metaphors like "spring," "rose," "sleep," "grave," looks in two opposite directions at once, and thus offers a choice between contraries. Like Milton in *Paradise Lost*, Vaughan shows that at first fallen man mistakes discord for concord, evil for good, and false regeneration for true. Once, however, the polarity between sin and regeneration is detected, poems such as "The Night" strike one as impressively cogent, rather than mystically rhapsodic. The recognition that where there seems to be concord, there is actually discord thus lays the groundwork for the second stage of *discordia concors*, the demonstration that what appear to be opposites are, in fact, united.

If "The Night" were isolated from the rest of *Silex Scintillans* and read without benefit of the parodic pattern of a false external nature imitating the inner spiritual world, the paradox of Nicodemus seeing the sun at midnight would surely be cited as simply an allusion to the traditional dark night of the soul. But recognition of a probable source never accounts for the success of any poem. And since Vaughan has condensed certain Janus-like metaphors into an exceedingly compact psychological shorthand throughout *Silex Scintillans*, "The Night" must be read next to the parodic pattern which these metaphors create. Then one may truly appreciate why in Vaughan's theory of knowledge midnight is the right and proper time to see the sun, Jesus Christ.

To attribute the virtues of day to the night sharply signals a reversal in moral value—a reversal directly linked to the poet's belief that nature is deceptive and seductive. Moreover, "The Night" is set in just such a context of unregeneration. Since metaphors of the visible world, like the "high-spring" of "Regeneration," counterfeit the invisible and spiritual, the poet is able to achieve regeneration poetically. Having first revealed discord amidst apparent concord, he then compares the regenerate and unregenerate halves of a metaphor to the larger parodic pattern of appearance masquerading as reality and the good, a pattern controlling the whole of *Silex Scintillans*. Then, within the context of a world that paints and lies, the poet transposes the traditional virtues of day into its opposite, and attributes goodness to the night. In this second stage of *discordia concors*, spiritual rebirth is thus accomplished by violently yoking the regenerate half of a metaphor with its spiritual counterpart, so that a "regenerate paradox" is created. In the unregenerate context of "The Night," the darkness of nature now corresponds to the inner, the good, and the spiritual. Therefore night is most appropriately yoked with the sun of heaven, Jesus Christ. Yoking of opposites is neither rhetorical flourish nor simply an allusion to the mystical dark night of the soul, but rather the final and necessary coincidence of opposites, a pattern which corresponds to Vaughan's underlying faith that through *discordia concors* souls may communicate not only with the dead, but find heaven as well. The appropriateness of the final conjunction persuades one that ("The Night" 49-54)

> There is in God (some say)
> A deep, but dazling darkness; As men here
> Say it is late and dusky, because they
>   See not all clear;
> O for that night! where I in him
> Might live invisible and dim.

Contrariety has again become regenerate unity in the "dazling darkness" of God—Vaughan's ultimate vision of *discordia concors*:[12]

Abide then with me, O thou whom my soul loveth! Thou Sun of righteousnesse with healing under thy wings arise in my heart; refine, quicken, and cherish it; make thy light there to shine in darknesse, and a perfect day in the dead of night.

FIVE

ANDREW MARVELL: UNITY IN MULTIPLICITY

The same desire to reconcile discord was as strong for Andrew Marvell when he was composing his best lyrics in the 1650s as it was for Donne when he wrote the *Anniversaries* forty years earlier,[1] but the poetic tactics have changed. In Marvell's lyrics we are able to pinpoint both the shift in *discordia concors* and in metaphysical wit from a violent yoking of opposites to the gentler unity in multiplicity, whose purpose is transcendent. In the attempt to judge Marvell's development of *discordia concors*, an interval of four decades becomes significant. Harold Toliver justly observes that "we do not expect to find a poet as modern as Marvell absorbing tradition without some awareness of his distance from it."[2] Indeed, Marvell seems intensely aware of this distance, and his poetry betrays the increasing difficulty of making those connections between extremes of human experience that draw the soul into a unified and coherent relationship with God and the invisible realm of spirit. And yet, paradoxically, the very difficulty of making those connections is exhibited not so much by the stylistically violent yoking of opposites evident in earlier metaphysical literature, as by the very ease of metaphor and wit. As Toliver says, "a peculiarly *distilled* feeling" does pervade the lyrics.[3]

By the 1650s it was more difficult than ever to use *discordia concors* as a transcendent yoking of opposites to bring "heaven hither" as Donne had in *The Second Anniversary*. One expects, therefore, that Marvell might approach such problems rather differently from John Donne or George Herbert, and in many distinctive ways he does.

The themes of Marvell's lyrics are the traditional ones of love, nature and art, body and soul, time and eternity, retirement and involvement, heaven and earth—to name but a few. The poems of the 1650s attempt to define the relationship between these antithetical pairs and, if possible, resolve them. Frequently, however, within a single poem they terminate in a stalemate of balanced contrariety. Marvell's resolution of opposites is literally dis-solution. To ease by death the tension that results from contrariety is an extreme response to life's problems, but in the lyrics annihilation *is* Marvell's answer to the horror of a discordant world. In secular poetry there is no way to transcend or transmute the ills that flesh and soul are heir to. Indeed, Marvell imitates with great precision the mind's experience in transient time; in time man is locked within conflicting and mixed emotions that pull in opposite directions at once. This is the bow of Heraclitus whose name is life, but whose work is death. Since bow or $βιός$ forms a pun with $βίos$, the word for life, it illustrates the paradox "that life and death are but two intertwining aspects of the same thing."[4] Like Damon the Mower, Marvell attempts to solve the dilemma of the earthly discordant concord; he searches in verse for ease, but the "cure" to contrariety is not easily found.

In the ostensibly secular lyrics, even more so than in Donne's *Songs and Sonnets*, for example, one witnesses perhaps an even greater difficulty for the poet to yoke together "the most heterogeneous ideas." Or, as sometimes happens, contraries *are* brought together, but they remain at strife, strained, and hostile in the Heraclitean pattern. In Marvell's religious verse, on the other hand, *discordia concors* succeeds through ecstatic dissolution, but this is not achieved by means of the violent yoking of opposites observed in Donne's *Second Anniversary*. Rather, one detects the reemergence in Marvell's verse of *discordia concors* as unity in multiplicity, whose aim is spiritual transcendence. This is a pattern which reconciles discord by emphasizing likeness rather than difference. The various patterns of *discordia concors* overlap, of course, but the violent and triumphant reversals so characteristic of early, and particularly Donnean, metaphysical wit have definitely begun to subside by the 1650s. Violent imagery still abounds in Marvell, but the metaphors are now become very dense and allusive, and the reconciliation of opposites is accomplished more gradually, as the reader begins to absorb the weight of accumulated value that certain words and metaphors carry. Despite a resistant opacity beneath the silvery surface, Donnean roughness and dramatic bravado have been smoothed away, to be replaced by that typical Marvellian translucence. Nevertheless, in spite of its evolution, the ultimately transcendent purpose of *discordia concors* remains unchanged for both Donne and Marvell: to close all divisions created by man's Fall: to restore lost harmonies and lost Edens. The manner in which each poet manipulates *discordia concors* necessarily varies, and in Marvell's distinctive development of the principle, metaphor and "annihilation" play a central role, a role that is appreciated only by a comparative study of certain lyrics.

In "A Dialogue, between The Resolved Soul, and Created Pleasure," Pleasure attempts to lure the Soul to rest here on earth among created delights: "On these downy Pillows lye, / . . . On these Roses strow'd so plain." But the Soul wisely answers that its "gentler Rest is on a Thought, / Conscious of doing what . . . [it] ought." Throughout, Soul and Pleasure are unalterably opposed. At the close the Chorus praises the Soul's admirable constancy:

> *Triumph, triumph, victorious Soul;*
> *The World has not one Pleasure more:*
> *The rest does lie beyond the Pole,*
> *And is thine everlasting Store.*

The pleasures of the Soul do indeed rest beyond the pole, beyond the outermost reaches of the mortal world. The very nature of the Soul's delight is its "*everlasting Store,*" its heavenly rest.[5] Recall Pleasure's attempt to persuade the Soul to recline "on these downy Pillows," but the Soul always knew its "gentler Rest" dwelt "*beyond the Pole.*" The dilemma for mortals is that on earth and in time Soul and Pleasure appear irreconcilable.

The debate continues in "A Dialogue between the Soul and Body." The Soul is imprisoned, "hung up, as 'twere, in Chains / Of Nerves, and Arteries, and Veins." Meanwhile the Body cries out in its own bondage, "O who shall me deliver whole, / From bonds of this Tyrannic Soul?" The suffering is further complicated because the Soul must endure the Body's ills, while the Body questions why it should tolerate the Soul's infirmities. The apparently contrarious and mutually detrimental activities of Soul and Body ironically join them in misery. The witty irony of the final stanza only underscores the discord between them. By pursuing its essential nature, each binds itself to its opposite, with almost unbearable results: the Soul is "fetter'd" (by lovely puns) "in Feet" and "manacled in Hands," while the Body is subject to the Soul's emotions and wit.[6]

> What but a Soul could have the wit
> To build me up for Sin so fit?
> So Architects do square and hew
> Green Trees that in the Forest grew.

The Soul's wit is analogous to the architect who destroys nature to build civilization and cities, but the worthy impulse to build is perverted. Since together Soul and Body only destroy one another, Marvell implies that they were happier far, if actually *far* apart. Death seems the only cure to their antagonism, but in life, how do Body and Soul separately pursue their own bliss when fettered and manacled?

Marvell was obsessed with the problem of Body and Soul on earth, and he probed it in the love lyrics. "To his Coy Mistress" verges upon the terrifying when it becomes obvious that death is the only answer to time and the lady's coyness. With exquisite irony Marvell satirizes the long-languishing Petrarchan lady who eludes, for what seems an eternity, her equally constant but anxious lover, who admits that "Had we but World enough, and Time, / This coyness Lady were no crime." But man does *not* have "World enough, and Time." The tone of the poem changes radically, once "Times winged

Charriot" hurries near, and the lover contemplates what constancy to an ethic of perpetually unfulfilled love means in an inconstant world. The urgency in the third stanza to "sport us while we may" becomes decidedly ominous as the man suggests they imitate "am'rous birds of prey," and "Rather at once our Time devour, / Than languish in his slow-chapt pow'r." As two lovebirds they would consume one another, and "tear . . . Pleasures with rough strife." The lover's solution to "Times winged Charriot" is death in the commonplace Renaissance sense of sexual death,[7] but Marvell gives the playful proposition a very sinister turn. Although the natural sun by which we tell time never stands still for any man, these witty lovers (like Phaeton) will try to make the sun run—in other words, they will attempt to create their own time.[8] And by their sexual annihilation they will give birth to a son indeed, but the lovers must also accept the fate of Phaeton. As Phaeton's chariot of the sun fiercely scorched the earth, so the lovers in their "Passions heat" ("The Garden" 25) must accept the "Deserts of vast Eternity" that stretch out endlessly before them. The invitation to love was initially based upon an argument to accept the exigencies of time, but to obey these pressures is ironically to gain the "Deserts of vast Eternity" which, in the logic of the argument, is the very thing they are trying to escape. The poem ends on the exultant note of the lover's rapturous prayer for a bright and fiery finish, but the certainty of ultimate extinction and "thy marble Vault" still chills his heated proposal. As in Shakespeare's Sonnet VII, exhortations to the young man to "get a son" by procreation do not suffice as a solution to the ravages of time.

"The Definition of Love" is not unlike "To his Coy Mistress" because death again provides the only answer to a love that essentially is neither dull nor sublunary:

> My Love is of a birth as rare
> As 'tis for object strange and high:
> It was begotten by despair
> Upon Impossibility.

As with the coy mistress, the nature of this love lies in the impossibility of its fulfillment:

> And yet I quickly might arrive
> Where my extended Soul is fixt,
> But Fate does Iron wedges drive,
> And alwaies crouds itself betwixt.

Like the unwanted chaperone, Fate's "Iron wedges" part the "Two perfect Loves; nor lets them close." The soul's whole effort is toward union with the object of its affection, but such union is impossible; the lovers are separated as much as the two poles are by the entire world, so that

> Unless the giddy Heaven fall,
> And Earth some new Convulsion tear;
> And, us to joyn, the World should all
> Be cramp'd into a *Planisphere*.

If union is to be achieved, the round world that separates them must be collapsed. The poem ends without resolution, however, on a note of perpetual longing. True, the lovers are bound by a "conjunction of the Mind," but their situation appears far from satisfactory; the only answer is, as in "To his Coy Mistress"—annihilation. In a very real sense, it is worldliness that separates the lovers, the wanton world that all men know after the Fall, and unless the world itself be destroyed, there seems no way to recover love's "birth" or origin (that is, the way love was before the Fall), nor love's berth, where it longs to return. This love is otherworldly, and the only way to reach that haven is through the death of all that separates the lover from "so divine a thing" as his "object strange and high."

The fallen world of nature that divides mankind from the object of his desire must be transcended or restored to Edenic simplicity, but as the curious pastoral figure of the Mower reveals, this is not easily achieved ("Mower's Song"):

> My Mind was once the true survey
> Of all these Medows fresh and gay;
> And in the greenness of the Grass
> Did see its Hopes as in a Glass.

Once the meadowland, which represents the world of nature, was a perfect reflection of man's mind, but that fellowship with nature was lost when woman entered the scene. The loss of companionship with the green fields and the obscure death of the Mower indicate the profound disturbance Juliana's advent brings ("The Mower to the Glo-Worms"):

> For She my Mind hath so displac'd
> That I shall never find my home.

Once the Mower's mind was *placed* in nature, and nature was its home. The question for mankind now becomes, of course, where *is* home? And where, indeed, is the mind's home?[9]

The other "Mower" poems provide clues. In "Damon the Mower" Damon sings

> With love of *Juliana* stung!
> While ev'ry thing did seem to paint
> The Scene more fit for his complaint.

This is his lament of unrequited love:

> Alas! I look for Ease in vain,
> When Remedies themselves complain.
> No moisture but my Tears do rest,
> Nor Cold but in her Icy Breast.

When he enjoyed the fellowship of the meadows, all nature had showered love on him:

> On me the Morn her dew distills
> Before her darling Daffadils.
> And, if at Noon my toil me heat,
> The Sun himself licks off my Sweat.
> While, going home, the Ev'ning sweet
> In cowslip-water bathes my feet.

Cast out from his natural home, Damon discovers his love for Juliana is not returned. She is inaccessible; her sunlike "scorching beams" are fierce and unkind, unlike those of the natural sun that gently licked the sweat from the Mower's back. Juliana's heats are clearly unnatural and harmful:

> This heat the Sun could never raise,
> Nor Dog-star so inflame's the dayes.
> It from an higher Beauty grow'th,
> Which burns the Fields and Mower both:
> Which mads the Dog, and makes the Sun
> Hotter than his own *Phaeton*.
> Not *July* causeth these Extremes,
> But *Juliana's* scorching beams.

"*Juliana's* scorching beams" cause both man and meadow to burn, but there is no cure for Damon except death:

> Only for him no Cure is found,
> Whom *Julianas* Eyes do wound.
> 'Tis death alone that this must do:
> For Death thou art a Mower too.

Like the typical Petrarchan woman, Juliana is inaccessible, full of "daunger," but her coyness has become indeed dangerous—her sun "beams" are "scorching," and her "Eyes do wound." The origin of Juliana's fierce and deathly rays apparently "from an higher Beauty grow'th." Sexual death might "cure" the Mower's passionate longing for Juliana but, like that star-crossed lover in "The Definition of Love," Damon's love is also "for object strange and high," "begotten by despair / Upon Impossibility." As a fierce and blazing sun, Juliana torments mankind rather than heals his wounds. She tempts the Mower to measure up to her "higher Beauty," but it is an ill-fated endeavor to follow Juliana.

The Mower's aspiration to unite with Juliana's "higher Beauty" is destined to failure, but the failure itself precisely outlines man's predicament. To cure the wound—Adam's wound of mortality—and to recover the lost fellowhip with nature thus become central preoccupations with Marvell. The radical disjunction between nature and the mind leads to various attempts to restore contrariety to harmony. One response is to reform nature, to make it correspond again with the mind. But any effort to yoke contraries in order to hasten the recovery of paradise is perverted, as is made clear in "The Mower against Gardens." After his own seduction, "Luxurious Man" seduced the rest of the world:

> And from the fields the Flow'rs and Plants allure,
> Where Nature was most plain and pure.
> He first enclos'd within the Gardens square
> A dead and standing pool of Air.

Like "Architects" who "square and hew / Green Trees that in the Forest grew," fallen man's enclosure of nature "within the Gardens square" results not in the restoration of Edenic harmony, but ironically in its very opposite, the "dead and standing pool of Air." Man's perversion of natural fertility creates only "uncertain and adult'rate fruit," a bawdy house of painted flowers, presided over by the safe and sexless eunuch. Statues of the gods set out to adorn the gardens finally only mock the artist, because "the *Gods* themselves" do not dwell "within the Gardens square," but in the "wild and fragrant Innocence" of "willing Nature." The attempt of art and worldly endeavor to enforce an order of higher beauty, to restore the simple innocence of that first garden in Eden, ends only in death and stagnation. And what "Luxurious Man" does not realize is that his tampering with physical nature is a vain and empty practice, because paradise is restored only through the work of time. To compute that time is the proper work of the "industrious Bee," as "The Garden" shows.

Although "The Garden" reveals that some reformation of "the errours of the Spring" ("The Picture of Little T. C. in a Prospect of Flowers") is possible, it also discloses pathetic attempts at reformation:

> How vainly men themselves amaze
> To win the Palm, the Oke, or Bayes;
> And their uncessant Labours see
> Crown'd from some single Herb or Tree,
> Whose short and narrow verged Shade
> Does prudently their Toyles upbraid;
> While all Flow'rs and all Trees do close
> To weave the Garlands of repose.

The hasty, worldly activities of man bring at best but a garland of leaves. "Crown'd from some single Herb or Tree," this "short and narrow verged Shade" proves a poor crown indeed that "does prudently upbraid their Toyles." Men are "amazed"—diverted from their proper pursuits. The world they inhabit *is* a maze itself, a labyrinth that entangles and traps; they go in circles, "But ever to no ends," like the nameless "stirrer" in Ben Jonson's "Cary-Morison Ode" (29-30).[10] All *is* vanity. All that bustle to find a little shade, a little repose! Worldly activity, Marvell is saying, creates a rather puny garden after all. If repose is truly wanted, he jokes, is it not better to retire to a real garden? "Society is all but rude," compared "To this delicious Solitude." The circle, or crown of glory, that worldly toil brings in stanza 1 is but the imperfect image of that better circle in the last stanza, the "fragrant Zodiack," in which "th' industrious Bee / Computes its time" (thyme) as the "wholsome Hours" of eternity.

It was not "rude" and unskilled "society," but God, the "skilful Gardner" and artist, who circumscribed the first garden in Eden. The initial stanzas of "The Garden" describe that golden age in the present tense, so that as readers we momentarily join the speaker in that joyous simplicity "Where willing Nature does to all dispence / A wild and fragrant Innocence" ("The Mower against Gardens" 33-34). The speaker is himself indistinguishable from nature. Each part of his being has its separate and appropriate ecstasy. The body has its proper bliss:

> What wond'rous Life in this I lead!
> Ripe Apples drop about my head;
> The Luscious Clusters of the Vine
> Upon my Mouth do crush their Wine.

The fullness of nature and its innocent sensuousness are entirely natural and good; its luxury is without taint of promiscuity.

The mind, too, has its particular ecstasy:

> Annihilating all that's made
> To a green Thought in a green Shade.

If "all that's made" means all that is created or artificial, then all art was once natural within the garden. "A green Thought in a green Shade" is, I believe, a condensed version of Damon's seeing his hopes reflected in the grass. At Juliana's advent (which represents a "fall" of some kind) Damon lost that cherished fellowship between his mind and the green grass of nature. Similarly, in "The Garden" the mind's ecstasy reflects a time in human history when the "green Thought" of mind corresponded to the "green Shade" of nature. Indeed, the mind was so thoroughly integrated within nature that "Thought" was "green"—nature's own best color. Thus, the mind was once its own garden or *hortus conclusus*, as Edward Tayler has demonstrated.[11] In "The Garden" "annihilation" is both creative and transcendent within the mind, and that is where the home must properly be. Tayler has rightly pointed out that "Marvell, unlike most of his modern readers, thought it possible to recover the lost harmony with Nature, which before the Fall man had possessed in the Garden."[12]

The soul likewise enjoys its own ecstasy, as it casts off the "Bodies Vest" to "glide" "into the boughs" where

> like a Bird it sits, and sings,
> Then whets, and combs its silver Wings;
> And, till prepar'd for longer flight,
> Waves in its Plumes the various Light.

Within the paradisical garden the soul is observed in its proper activity—preparation for the eventual journey to heaven's bower. The soul is patience itself; it sits and sings until the time is ripe for flight.

In stanza 8 these ecstasies initially appear shattered; the abrupt change in tenses signals that such pleasures occurred in the past—not in the present:

> Such was that happy Garden-state
> While Man there walk'd without a Mate:
> After a Place so pure, and sweet,
> What other Help could yet be meet!

It would have been far more "help," Marvell sarcastically implies, had Adam never *met* Eve, his erstwhile "helpmeet fit." Here, as in the "Mower" poems, man's purity, his wholesomeness, his integrity, and repose within the first earthly garden were "on a sudden lost, / Defac't, deflow'r'd, and now to Death devote" (*Paradise Lost* 9.900-01) through the advent of woman and sin. Originally Adam named the trees and all creation by their true names, according to their essential nature. After the Fall trees were "known" by girls' names wantonly carved in the bark by their lovers. But the speaker shares Adam's propensity for nomenclature:

> Fair Trees! where s'ere your barkes I wound,
> No Name shall but your own be found.

All nature had been perverted at the Fall: lasciviously Apollo chased Daphne and Pan raced after the nymph Syrinx. But in the garden of the mind that Marvell's wit creates, these postlapsarian activities are untwisted so that Apollo chases

Daphne that "she might Laurel grow," and Pan chases Syrinx "Not as a Nymph, but for a Reed." In the mind's garden the gods *do* dwell, because all is become natural. " 'Tis" *not* "all enforc'd" as it was in the stagnant gardens of "Luxurious Man." Here the pursuits of the gods, like those of the speaker and reader, are momentarily neither luxurious nor wanton, but entirely wholesome and innocent. At first, however, with our lapsed and fallen minds we read these changes in the traditional mythology as inversions and witty jokes—and only later as they actually are—the restoration through literalization, if only for a brief few stanzas, of an ideal world like Eden. The ecstatic quality of stanzas 5-7 is that possible only in the world of innocent nature, the world where, as the other lyrics tell us, art has no place unless it be nature's art. In stanza 7 the vision of Edenic repose collapses as both woman and time intrude.

The last stanza is critical because it reveals how woman and time provide the way back into bliss. The great allusiveness of Marvellian metaphor permits speculation to expand. The "skilful Gardner" (unlike that other gardener "Luxurious Man") whose innocent art created that "happy Garden-state," is the figure of God, but Marvell has himself imitated that very garden within the circular structure of his poem, and within his mind.

Like the first "gardner" Marvell has drawn his verse into a circle that tells time; the poem is, as he says, a "Dial new." Equally so, it is a "fragrant Zodiack" because it is actually a floral sundial that tells the observer the hours, days, seasons, and years. This garland of flowers and spices belittles the "uncessant Labours" of men who vainly run the race for worldly fame to be "Crown'd from some single Herb or Tree." Expressing a similar thought, Donne prays in *La Corona* that his "muses white sincerity" be not rewarded "with a vile crowne of fraile bayes," but with

> what thy thorny crowne gain'd, that give mee,
> A crowne of Glory, which doth flower alwayes;
> The ends crowne our workes, but thou crown'st our ends,
> For, at our end begins our endlesse rest.[13]

These lines underscore important questions for Marvell. What constitutes worthy endeavors? What ends? What rest? Time? The answer is suggested within the last stanza, especially in the metaphors of the "milder Sun" and "th' industrious Bee." Not only is the bee bucolic, as Rosalie Colie declares in "*My Ecchoing Song*," but indeed it is "*the* georgic insect."[14] But further, I think Marvell is alluding particularly to Virgil, because in the *Georgics* there are two kinds of bees: one decidedly lazy and wicked; "others gleam, and flash in splendour, their bodies all ablaze and flecked with equal drops of gold. This is the nobler breed; from this, in the sky's due season, you will strain sweet honey."[15] The industry of Marvell's bee is well spent—not "In busie Companies of Men"—but in the computation of time and the "sky's due season." The "wholsome Hours" are literally thyme, as A. H. King notes.[16] All true labor in the garden is properly directed toward gaining "the Garlands of repose." Busi-ness is restlessness, the very opposite of repose and rest. "Expense of spirit in a waste of shame" is not time well spent, but the proper computation of "wholsome Hours" brings solitude and repose. When time is computed as thyme—within the "fragrant Zodiack"—it adds up to or completes the circle and becomes "wholsome" indeed because it is both perfect and entire, an emblem of the eternity it foreshadows. Only by laboring well within the natural cycle of "thyme" does it turn at last to eternity; paradise cannot be rushed.

The "industrious Bee" who "computes its time" or judges time as eternity is guided in his earthly endeavors, not by the "Passions heat" of Petrarchan lovers, nor by the lovers in "To his Coy Mistress" who would depose the sun and create their own son, nor yet by the "scorching beams" of that fierce sun Juliana, but by the "milder Sun." Toliver appreciates that "the sun is thus 'milder' in contrast to Juliana-Phaeton suns," but he seems to consider the "milder Sun" as entirely natural: "Time and eternity," he says, "are reconciled: the impregnating sun creates the 'tyme' in which the bee works."[17] Frank Kermode believes "the sun is 'milder' because in this zodiac of flowers fragrance is substituted for heat."[18] I believe, however, that it is only by seeing in the "milder Sun" a figure of

Christ,[19] "th' Almighty Sun" of "On a Drop of Dew," that "The Garden" fulfills its purpose as a sign and testament that man's wandering and "amazed" mind will in time wander back to paradise, a paradise that was glimpsed momentarily within the *hortus mentis* of stanzas 5-8.

Throughout the lyrics the sun, as well as numerous other words and actions, reappears frequently. The repetition is significant, especially when it is evident that the connotation of these words varies extremely according to the context. These variations are, I think, intentional and meant to be observed, because they force us as readers to imitate Marvell's use of *discordia concors*. Only by comparing and contrasting certain words and events as they appear in different, but thematically related contexts, do they become symbolical. Some even become contraries when they are compared, thus assuming the nature of paradox. Marvell believed that contrariety was at the heart of the universe, and that its resolution depended upon God in the fullness of time.

In the particular instance of the word "sun," comparison and contrast has previously revealed such a diversity of moral value that the true function of the "milder Sun" can hardly be merely natural. A significant ambiguity in the use of "it" and "its" also signals the appropriateness of a deeper meaning:

> Where from above the milder Sun
> Does through a fragrant Zodiack run;
> And, as it works, th' industrious Bee
> Computes its time as well as we.

If "as it works, th' industrious Bee / Computes its time" is interpreted as the *bee* computes its time, then one tends to forget that "it" and "its" can just as easily refer to the "milder Sun." Once this grammatical ambiguity is perceived, then clearly the bee's time (as well as ours) *is*, in fact, the milder Sun's time: the two have become one. Our time is only made whole in Christ, and the "milder Sun" foreshadows the time of Christ.

Like Milton's Christ, the "mild Judge and Intercessor both," who entered Eden while the sun set "in Western cadence low," to judge our errant first parents (*P.L.* 10.96, 92), the "milder Sun" in "The Garden" intimates the eventual turning of time into the sweetness of eternity. When time has run its course the ecstasies that faded in stanza 8 shall become perpetual. Then man shall wear the true "Garlands of repose," and enjoy "*the rest* [*that*] *does lie beyond the Pole,* / *And is thine everlasting Store*" ("A Dialogue, between The Resolved Soul, and Created Pleasure"). Until then "The Garden" remains a complex metaphor—simultaneously of innocent bliss in Eden, of transitory bliss within the mind's garden, and the final bliss of heaven where "then at last our bliss / Full and perfect is" ("On the Morning of Christ's Nativity" 165-66). When the circle is summed, then shall good men, by their good industry on earth, having run the good race, return home to rest in heaven with the Son, Jesus Christ. As George Herbert wrote:[20]

> Sure thou wilt joy, by gaining me
> To flie home like a laden bee
> Unto that hive of beams
> And garland-streams.

Virgil's bees were as wise:[21]

Some have taught that the bees have received a share of the divine intelligence, and a draught of heavenly ether; for God, they say, pervades all things, earth and sea's expanse and heaven's depth; from Him the flocks and herds, men and beasts of every sort draw, each at birth, the slender stream of life; yea, unto Him all beings thereafter return, and, when unmade, are restored; no place is there for death, but, still quick, they fly unto the ranks of the stars, and mount to the heavens aloft.

At the end of "The Garden" we have circled round to a situation similar to that which the Puritans experienced in "Bermudas," as they gratefully sang God's praises while rowing toward the island of Bermuda. In the seventeenth century Bermuda was thought Edenic—an island, Marvell says, of "eternal Spring." An island of eternal spring has neither harsh winters nor mortal failings; mutability and time have not ruined its song.

The full-to-bursting, luscious fruit in Bermuda echoes stanza 5 of "The Garden":

> What wond'rous Life in this I lead!
> Ripe Apples drop about my head.

In "The Garden" the body's enjoyment of such pleasures is momentary; in "Bermudas" the rowers have been "led . . . through the watry Maze" by God; they have escaped the vanity of men who "themselves amaze / To win the Palm, the Oke, or Bayes," but they are only on the verge of Bermuda's garden paradise, and not yet within it. They have glimpsed its perfection, but like the "industrious Bee," they too must wait until time becomes eternity. Only good faith and good works bring that sweetness. Meanwhile they rightly sing God's praise, "Till it arrive at Heavens Vault," and as they sing "to guide their Chime, / With falling Oars they kept the time." The "falling Oars" signal the *beat,* while the "time" makes up the *measure* of their song. Rowing and singing reflect their proper earthly activity: they *keep time* (just as the "industrious Bee / Computes its time as well as we") until it becomes eternity, and paradise can be reentered and fully enjoyed. Again like the bee, they do not try to speed up time, nor do they attempt to reform time; they *accept* time because they know it holds eternity.

In both "Bermudas" and "The Garden" Marvell has skillfully prepared our responses, so that for a fleeting moment we share the vision of the "happy Garden-state." Then suddenly the vision vanishes, and we realize that this paradise was actually in the past ("Such was that happy Garden-state") or yet in the future. In "Bermudas" we are again caught up in the present tense:

> He hangs in shades the Orange bright,
> Like golden Lamps in a green Night.
> And does in the Pomegranates close
> Jewels more rich than *Ormus* shows.
> He makes the Figs our mouths to meet;
> And throws the Melons at our feet.

But when we read the last four lines of "Bermudas" it is clear that "this eternal Spring" is not to be possessed completely until spring becomes eternal:

> Thus sung they, in the *English* boat,
> An holy and a chearful Note,
> And all the way, to guide their Chime,
> With falling Oars they kept the time.

The vision of "eternal Spring" *was* the song that now helps men keep the time as they row toward paradise. In both poems one feels the sudden shock of hiatus as the vision recedes and earthly time intrudes once more. One feels, too, Marvell's inability to transcend this world triumphantly through a violent yoking of opposites—in a flash to turn chaos and mortality into coherence and immortality as Donne had in *The Second Anniversary*; Marvell has beguiled us with the vision of bliss and then apparently withdrawn it, leaving us to our mortality, and yet he carefully lodges within his allusive metaphors a way back into bliss, imperfectly now, but perfectly later. Yet the business of living well, of computing time organically in the natural world as thyme, and of running the good race, seems a more acute preoccupation with Marvell than with Donne, who appears less content to "keep time," preferring to "leap the present age" to heaven whenever possible.

For Marvell the irony of the human predicament is perhaps even more intense in 1650 than for Donne at the turn of the century; it is softened only by the belief that time can be reckoned and reckoned with. If man no longer sees his hopes reflected in the grass because mortality has no spring, still a single hope remains. There is, of course, no hope for the lovers in "To his Coy Mistress" who would in passion create their own son, while deposing the natural sun and running his race for him. The only hope lies in the spring of resurrection—in the "Almighty Sun" of "On a Drop of Dew," who died to repair man's "errours of the Spring." In the allusive pastoral kind Marvell has repeatedly stated that death and annihilation provide the only cure for man's displaced and "double . . . Mind," and the unusual heats that Juliana brought into the world. It is, however, uniquely Christian pastoral that answers the "dead ends" of pagan pastoral, for it alone provides Christ, the sole sun and Son, who as alpha and omega can reconcile man's "double . . . Mind" with the oneness of God and bring it home again.

In "The Coronet" it becomes evident that annihilation depends upon grace. The poet has offered a "chaplet" of flowers and verses (both posies) to redress the wrong of Christ's wearing a crown of thorns. Ironically, however, the serpent has wormed his way into the chaplet, "With wreaths of Fame and Interest," making it an unfit, vain offering. The poem ends in dilemma: either Christ must shatter the chaplet to destroy the serpent, thus annihilating the poet's good as well, or he must extract and annihilate the devil in an act of grace. Either way the irony cuts very deep. Man's wish to re-dress or reclothe Christ with a garland of flowers and poems is an understandable longing, but it is Christ's grace that redresses man, in every sense of the word. Man's salvation from sin depends upon God's grace—even the gift of poetry is divinely inspired. And finally it is Christ himself who shall redress man in "the robe of righteousness" (Isaiah 61:10). It is man who is in need of redress, not Christ.

In "On a Drop of Dew" grace becomes the means to Christian annihilation. Death *is* the only cure, but not in the sense that Damon the Mower thought. Within the paradox of Christian extasis and annihilation, one dies to live. Annihilation can "peece the circle" that ends in God. It is a conventional theme that only in the world of mortal nature is there no resurrection. Henry Howard, Earl of Surrey, for instance, sadly witnessed the renewal of all life in springtime save his own:[22]

> And thus I see among these pleasant thinges
> Eche care decayes, and yet my sorow springes.

Unlike the perennial flowers of nature, there is no spring for mankind except through the grace of Christ, who brought promise of rebirth and restoration.

"On a Drop of Dew" must be considered in greater detail because it solves the dilemma of the lyrics that have in various ways probed love for a higher beauty and the possibility of the mind's return to its proper home. Here, at last, annihilation *is* a satisfactory answer and death *is* a cure.

Critics have tended to read the poem in three sections: lines 1-18 are "about" the dew, lines 19-36 are "about" the soul, and lines 37-40 are "about" that "belatedly" introduced image of the manna.[23] In this reading the first two segments are perfectly symmetrical, but the final four lines resist analysis, which implies that Marvell created an exquisite bubble in the initial sections, but blew it in the last.

Unquestionably Marvell does set up three sections, but then he simultaneously asserts their unity and circularity: dew, soul, and manna are three things that paradoxically are one. The natural cycle of the dew's condensation and anticipated evaporation occupies the first eighteen lines without any overt mention of the soul. In the second eighteen lines the soul parallels the dew in its cycle of life, death, and hoped-for resurrection. The third section (37-40) ostensibly concerns the manna that fell from heaven.

Closer inspection, however, uncovers significant ambiguities that weaken the rigidity of a tripartite structure. Line 19, for example, which introduces the soul, begins with the correlative "so":

> So the Soul, that Drop, that Ray
> Of the clear Fountain of Eternal Day.

Such a comparison of the dew to the soul would seem to indicate the presence of an understood "like as" (or "as") within the initial eighteen lines. The as-so relationship makes it more difficult to separate the two sections.

Ambiguities in the final lines further weaken a tertiary reading. The verbs, especially, act unpredictably. "Did . . . destil" is past tense, signifying completed action, but the next verb deviates from the expected "did run," and instead, a present participle, "dissolving" (suggesting perpetual motion), is wedged into the present indicative verb "does . . . run." Sir Thomas Browne clarifies both Marvell's motive for distorting tenses and the function of the "Manna's sacred Dew" when he asks, "who can speake of eternitie without a soloecisme, or thinke thereof without an extasie?"[24] With a solecism, implicitly, one *can* speak of eternity. By yoking together past and present verbs, Marvell jolts us into Browne's perception that "in eternity there is no distinction of Tenses" (*R.M.* 1.11). We are now ready to conjecture whether the appearance of the manna was simply an event completed in the biblical past or whether it also occurs outside man's ordinary conception of tenses, in the eternal present. If it is such an eternal event, the meaning of the "Manna's sacred Dew" may be shared by poet and reader alike.[25] Marvell's confusion of tenses has been most appropriate, since "On a Drop of Dew" is very much about timelessness. The first thirty-six lines have led to the expectation of rising; the ecstatic quality of the last four lines stems from the anticipation of resurrection into eternity.

Line 37 begins with another ambiguity that detracts from a strictly tertiary interpretation. The word "such" looks in two opposite directions at once; it can refer to the previous thirty-six lines as well as to the subsequent four. Thus the dew-soul entity of the initial thirty-six lines may act as the subject of the verb "did . . . destil," which makes the "Manna's sacred Dew" its direct object. This means that the dew-soul did distil or cause the sacred dew to fall to earth. "Destil" is of course derived from the Latin *distillare*, "to drop." Alternatively, the "Manna's sacred Dew" did distil or was the source of (compare the link to the "clear Fountain of Eternal Day"), or caused the first thirty-six lines (the dew-soul), which are themselves imaginatively circular, to fall in drops from heaven to earth.

Moreover, the tripartite structural analysis fails to account entirely for the way in which the Marvellian wit functions, because, most importantly, the basic analogy is between something from nature (the dew) and something from heaven (the soul). Immediately Marvell subtly implies that nature is like heaven. Comparing small things with greatest, or simply comparing what seem to be contraries, Marvell demonstrates that the difference is not in kind but only in degree. Unlike the earlier metaphysical poets, and like the later Milton, Marvell here minimizes the distance and difference between earth and heaven. In the *Sermons* Donne accentuates the dichotomies in life, and dwells at length upon the misery of humanity and its fate of worms and dust. Only after he has drawn out his theme to its outermost extremes does he yoke and transform the whole of mortality into radiant bliss. Marvell is not saying in his metaphors that nature or earth *is* heaven, but he is saying that in postlapsarian life one cannot readily distinguish between the two. If nature seems at odds with heaven, it is only because paradoxically they correspond with one another. Before 1667 Milton was agonizing over the same problem in *Paradise Lost*. Raphael reveals both the problem and its solution (5.571-76):

> what surmounts the reach
> Of human sense, I shall delineate so,
> By lik'ning spiritual to corporal forms,
> As may express them best, though what if Earth
> Be but the shadow of Heav'n, and things therein
> Each to other like, more than on Earth is thought?

In other words, human understanding grasps the heavenly by analogy, by comparison of the natural to the supernatural or heavenly.[26] Within the orb of the natural dew the circle of the heavenly soul is reflected. In line 19 "soul" is followed by an appositional phrase, "that Drop, that Ray." By placing "soul" in such a construction Marvell maneuvers likeness to the point of identity. And yet, although dew and soul must seem contraries, just as nature and heaven do, at length they will be reconciled within the greater circle of God. There are hints. When he places "ray" in apposition with "soul," a backwards glance is cast at the "warm Sun" of the natural world of the dew, at the same time that a forward look anticipates the "Glories [which happen to be circles of light] of th' Almighty Sun" in heaven.

The circle that dew and soul form is paradoxical: it is "both the object, and the wit" as Donne says in *The Second Anniversary* (442). It is the "figure" that unveils the poet's intention of delineating the human soul by "lik'ning spiritual to corporal," that is, by likening soul to dew, and heavenly to earthly. Like God, that "skilful Geometrician," who with his golden compass created the world in circular shape, Marvell chose a circle to reveal his wit through *discordia concors*: for "nature is not at variance with art, nor art with nature;

... all things are artificiall; for nature is the Art of God."[27] Thus, within the circle of this poem we may, as Sir Thomas Browne says, "suck Divinity from the flowers of nature." In other words, we may "see" the heavenly soul within that "little Globes Extent," the natural dew, and within both we may see God.

The dew itself is fundamentally paradoxical. When it first appears, it is markedly human; it wishes, it fears, it trembles; and yet, the soul has not been mentioned explicitly. But readers imaginatively supply it, as so often required in metaphysical poetry. The "Orient Dew" is a complex metaphor—it is both real and natural, as well as symbolical of that supernatural entity the human soul. In one word, "dew," heaven and earth meet. As Dr. Johnson wrote, "Wit . . . may be . . . considered as a kind of *discordia concors*; a combination of dissimilar images, or discovery of occult resemblances in things apparently unlike."[28]

From above, this paradoxical dew has dropped to earth, "Into the blowing Roses," the terrestrial garden of the senses, but there it slights "the purple flow'r." Turning away on every side it

> Round in its self incloses:
> And in its little Globes Extent,
> Frames as it can its native Element.

Within the orbit of its being, the dew confines the essential purity retained from sky and heaven. Aloof, "careless of its Mansion new," the dew evidently prefers its former mansion, the Lord's house in heaven. Patently unhappy, fearful "lest it grow impure," the dew rolls on the surface of "the blowing Roses." These roses are probably swaying in the garden breeze; they are also undoubtedly blooming in voluptuous crimson glory, but they may also carry an additional feeling of excess, of too-blooming, even to the extent of tainted. Such a reading is supported by the disdain the dew exhibits toward the world of the "purple flow'r." One is reminded of "The Mower against Gardens," in which "Luxurious Man" "with strange perfumes . . . did the Roses taint." I do not wish to equate the "blowing Roses" of "On a Drop of Dew" with those in

"The Mower against Gardens." The atmosphere of the former poem is much more allusive, and it would be a mistake to press "the attar from the rose"[29] in order to create a little allegory. It is true, however, that within the diffuse aura of sexuality and *volupté*, Marvell exploits the conventional argument between body and soul. While preserving the platonic language that places body and nature lower than soul and heaven, Marvellian wit joins them in complex metaphor. In *Paradise Lost* (6.176) Milton's Abdiel asserts a similarly complex vision, in which "God and Nature bid the same."

Chastely the dew "Shines with a mournful Light; / Like its own Tear." The dew is at once mourner and mourned for, because it remembers (etymologically "mourn" means "remember") "the clear [from the Latin adjective *clarus*, "light"] Region where 'twas born." The dew "shines" like a mirror wherein can be seen a dark light indeed, but simultaneously there is a latent expectation that "the warm Sun [will] pitty its Pain," that its loss will be restored and its cycle completed. Having come with the "orient" sun, the fallen dew wishes to rise ("orient" is derived from the Latin *oriri*, "to rise") and return to its home with the sun. Similarly, because the dew is also supernatural, one can see in the "warm Sun" an adumbration of the "Almighty Sun." Moreover, in the seventeenth century Christ was called "Oriens" and identified with the sun. In a sermon Donne announces Christ's advent: "*Ecce vir, Oriens nomen ejus, Behold him, whose name is the East.*"[30]

It is now more apparent that Christ as "Manna's sacred Dew" and "th' Almighty Sun" are both prefigured in the "Orient Dew." Everything in the poem—dew, soul, manna's sacred dew, Christ, sun—falls to rise. There are many smaller circles within "On a Drop of Dew," but the circle of God is all-encompassing. The poem moves in a circuit from "orient" sun to "Almighty Sun." The orient sun of morning sets in Christ the Son, but again it rises as Christ does in the east. One can now better understand why the "mournful Light" of the dew is both dark and bright: it shines with mourning light *and* morning (orient) light. Dark has the potential of light, of rising, and of resurrection. At once the dew symbolizes all souls that wander throughout the earthly desert toward heaven's promised land, while it foreshadows an end to their wandering when, like Christ the orient sun, they too rise heavenwards.

In line 19 the dew is at last openly compared to the soul. The soul, or supernatural dew, in its course of life, death, and longed-for rebirth, deprecates its stay on earth. It slights "the humane flow'r" or body, and rejects "the sweet leaves and blossoms green." Echoing platonic theory, the soul recollects "its own Light," remembering an earlier existence in heaven. Like the dew the soul recollects or gathers itself around, and "Frames as it can its native Element." If we "compare / Small things with greatest" (*Paradise Regained* 4.563-64),[31] the art of the dew creates a little globe, or microcosm, that reflects the entire world. Similarly, the art of the soul, "in its pure and circling thoughts," frames a "figure" so coyly "wound" that "Every way it turns away." This "figure" is, of course, a circle—a circle that is both soul and dew and the poem itself. Within its perfect form these elements express "The greater Heaven in an Heaven less." There is no difference in kind, only in degree. The "world" may well be excluded, but paradoxically the macrocosm is seen within the microcosmic circle, for earth has become heavenly: "The whole world before thee is . . . as a drop of the morning dew that falleth down upon the earth" (Wisdom 11:22). Marvell thus bridges the platonic dichotomies exploited throughout the poem:

> Dark beneath, but bright above:
> Here disdaining, there in Love.

Within the circle of *discordia concors* that is both dew and soul and Christ, Marvell fuses body and soul, heaven and earth, dark and bright, and shows how disdaining can be a kind of love, just as nature is the art of God.

The resolution of the entire poem, however, hinges upon the final four lines which complete the circle. In line 37 the metaphor of the "Manna's sacred Dew" is introduced—"belatedly"—if Pierre Legouis is correct. It is, nevertheless, a metaphor that is implicitly foreshadowed. Exodus 16 reveals that manna was heavenly bread—small, white, and round—given to the Jews while they wandered in the wilderness toward the promised land. The dew that became manna was a miracle, a sign of God's grace and love for his Chosen People. In John (6:32, 51) Christ reinterprets the meaning of manna: "Moses gave you not that bread from heaven; but my Father giveth you the true bread from heaven." It is Christ himself who is "the living bread which came down from heaven: if any man eat of this bread, he shall live forever." Manna was thus an anticipation of Christ's coming to earth to die for man's sins that mankind might live in the promised land of paradise.

In the scriptural commentaries dew (Latin *ros*) signifies divine grace and the Holy Spirit.[32] Manna is repeatedly linked with the body of Christ and the mystery of the Eucharist.[33] In the *Allegoriae in universam Sacram Scripturam* Rabanus Maurus writes, for example, that "manna est corpus Christi,"[34] and in the *Enarrationis super Deuteronomium* he declares, "Manna enim de coelo datum significat carnem Christi. 'Ego sum,' inquit, 'panis vitae, qui de coelo descendit' (Joan. VI)."[35]

Metaphorical interpretation of Scripture was entirely traditional. It is only we today who regularly fail to respond to the typological import of so many words and figures. In the emblem book *Parthenia sacra* (Rouen, 1633), Henry Hawkins makes explicit what Marvell leaves implicit (p. 65):

Since the Sonne God of a litle graine of mustard sayes: *The kingdome of heaven is like to a graine of mustard-seed etc.* me thinks, I might say as wel: *The kingdome of heaven is like to a drop of Deaw*: For the *Saviour* of the world, who is the graine of mustard-seed, is likewise this same rich drop of *Deaw*.

In the *Holy Pictures of the mysticall Figures of the most holy Sacrifice and Sacrament of the Eucharist* (n.p., 1619), the Jesuit Lewis Richome describes the role of Christ both as manna and Eucharist, in terms very like *discordia concors*. God is the great harmonizer who brings all discords together:[36]

Is not then this divine Mystery [the Eucharist] an abridgment of Gods wonders? . . . Hee hath made appeare his greatness two wayes, the one in making of wonders apart, the other, which is the more divine, in assembling them together. As a Musition, that not onely knows to set for single voyces, but also hath the arte, and the grace of setting many parts together, and to delight the eare with a sweet harmony, composed of divers voyces well accorded. After that he had shewed himselfe wonderfull in the production of a thousand creatures, he made man, as an abridgement of them all. . . . God did all these miracles—but the greatest was his sacrifice—containing alone the abridgement of all the wonders. . . . True marke and signe of his greatnesse; true Manna, bearing the name of wonder; true bread, descended from heaven; true gift.

In this "sweet and well agreeing harmony" Richome concludes that "this combination surpasseth all wonder, for God and Nature are heere combined" (p. 126).

Even without special knowledge of the traditional symbolisms of manna and dew, readers may imaginatively complete the thought suggested in Marvell's poem. The cycle that brings dew to earth and souls to bodies may be likened to the Hebrews' forty years of wandering in the wilderness and to the forty lines of verse. While the "Orient Dew" waits (as natural dew) "Till the warm Sun pitty its Pain, / And to the Skies exhale it back again," the soul (as supernatural dew) also waits on earth, figuratively in the desert, but "ready to ascend" to heaven, the Canaan or promised land of souls. It waits until Christ, the "Almighty Sun," pity its pain and bring it to heaven again. As Jews in their exodus saw in the manna God's grace and promise of a new home, so readers may "see" figured in the "Manna's sacred Dew" not only their own soul, but also a sign of Christ's merciful mission.

Like the dew that was both natural and supernatural, so the "Manna's sacred Dew" is another Janus word that splits in two opposite directions at once. Even its form is double: it is "Congeal'd on Earth," but "does, dissolving, run / Into the Glories of th' Almighty Sun." Were it not for the pun on "sun" and "Son" it might be easier to anchor the "sacred Dew" solely to a mundane role, but even then the biblical background and the adjective "sacred" insist that it is a special degree of dew. All may now be considered in terms of dew: natural dew, soul as supernatural dew, and Christ as "sacred Dew": of kind the same, but differing in degree. Although each is not equivalent to the other, clearly they are one in a unique sense—of one kind, but three degrees. As Wallace Stevens wrote, "Identity is the vanishing-point of resemblance."[37]

The "Manna's sacred Dew" is central to our appreciation of the poem, for only by seeing in the falling manna an unmistakable anticipation of Christ's descent to earth—the sacrifice of the Son to ransom man's soul, so that like the "Orient Dew" it may rise and be resurrected to heaven—only then is it evident that to be fulfilled and completed, both cycles of natural and supernatural dew must undergo annihilation and absorption into the circle of God. Only in "dissolving" (death) does one "run" into that circle and so live. Donne makes a similar observation: "That which seems to be our dissolution, (our death) is the strongest *band* of this union [with God]."[38]

From the very first line of "On a Drop of Dew" Marvell has bid us "see" the human soul and finally God within the "little Globes Extent" of dew and poem. The dew "shines" darkly with its "mournful Light" because "now we see [God] through a glass darkly" (1 Cor. 13:12). But as we have a sign in the circle of the "Manna's sacred Dew," we shall in time see God face to face as he is in his essence. If we speculate aright in the glass or mirror of the dew,[39] we understand that eventually we "run / Into the Glories of th' Almighty Sun," Jesus Christ. Understanding man's fate in time permits us to keep the time on earth until we reenter paradise, man's best home.

Thus, Marvell's inability to yoke "the most heterogeneous ideas" together in order to transcend earthly discord prepared the way for his vision of *discordia concors* as unity in multiplicity, based upon a figural view of history in which all time and nature are organized typologically. In this version of *discordia concors*, earthly imperfection may be "computed," reckoned with, and endured, because every figure—whether soul, dew, or manna—anticipates its fulfillment in time: each awaits perfection in the "Almighty Sun." As time becomes timeless and nature supernatural, all divisions initiated at the Fall close in perpetual harmony.

SIX

JOHN MILTON: OPPOSITES AND MULTIPLICITY RESOLVED

When the twelve books of *Paradise Lost* initially appeared in the second edition of 1674, Milton straddled two different worlds: he looked back to the more typically astringent metaphysical style of yoking together "the most heterogeneous ideas," at the same time that he looked forward to the reemergence of *discordia concors* as a strictly classical, nontranscendent, Horatian pattern of unity in multiplicity, in which a wise and kindly monarch blends and balances the discordant elements within the circle of his realm.

Although not a Donnean yoking of opposites, the Miltonic simile may be associated with the more metaphysical manner of *discordia concors*, in which opposites are joined. Unlike Donne, who is occasionally able to transcend earthly discord to heaven's concord by violently fusing opposites that resist logical conjunction, Milton is unable to go beyond "the field of this world"[1] by the same means. To transcend earth, Milton finally dissolves the violent discord within similes by placing them within the framework of the all-encompassing Christianized pattern of *discordia concors* as unity in multiplicity. Then, like Marvell in "On a Drop of Dew," Milton reveals that heaven is restored when time becomes eternity.

Despite the fact that all similes, or metaphorical comparisons, involve difference as well as sameness, Milton is distinctive in equally emphasizing both at once. Critics, on the other hand, have tended to weight either similarity or difference, so that unwittingly their readings are distorted. It is therefore not surprising to discover that although the Miltonic simile is one of the most frequently repeated stylistic devices in *Paradise Lost*, its very relevance and function have been disputed for nearly three hundred years. In this century the anti-Miltonists have leveled broadsides at the similes for a variety of faults. T. S. Eliot, for example, sarcastically deplores "the happy introduction of so much extraneous matter. Any writer, straining for images of hugeness, might have thought of the whale, but only Milton could have included the anecdote of the deluded seamen without our wanting to put a blue pencil through it."[2] And F. R. Leavis sputters that "Miltonic similes don't focus one's perception of the relevant, or sharpen definition in any way."[3] Defenders of Milton's "grand style" have, however, emphatically shown that the simile is never wholly decorative; that its purpose is not merely to please or to provide relief to the sweated brow of the reader, but is intimately related to the overall unity of the epic. At the same time that they defend its appositeness, however, the critics have only partially disclosed the character and function of the simile.

In "The Miltonic Simile" James Whaler demonstrates with something like mathematical equations that the similes are reduceable to sets of logical formulae.[4] By pictorially placing the thing compared (tenor) next to the comparison (vehicle) and arranging the shared resemblances in order of textual appearance, as in the simile below (*P.L.* 2.707-11), Whaler understandably concludes that "homologation rather than heterogeneity between the terms is the rule."

Whaler's close reading sharply underscores his belief that the analogies drawn are remarkably pertinent.

Whaler's depiction of simile formulae also illustrates Milton's use of prolepsis, a rhetorical device that anticipates events to come. Because the immediate context is often insufficient to clarify the full implications of a simile, analogies that for-

```
                    Satan ─────────┬───────── Comet
                          fiery radiance
                                   │
                            enormousness
                                   │
                    ominousness of impending calamity
```

"The infernal serpent" is the poet's characterization of Satan at the very beginning of the poem.	"Ophiucus" means "holder of serpent"; therefore a comet, assimilated to Satan, most appropriately fires the length of Ophiucus.
Always associated with the nothern quarter of Heaven.	"arctic sky."—To make his homologue Milton puts Ophiucus in the North, but only with considerable astronomical freedom.

merly appeared inapt and digressive may now be read more meaningfully through prolepsis. The leviathan simile, for example, which Eliot found so "extraneous," is now alarmingly direct and to the point. Satan, like leviathan (1.201-08),

> God of all his works
> Created hugest that swim th' Ocean stream:
> Him haply slumb'ring on the *Norway* foam
> The Pilot of some small night-founder'd Skiff,
> Deeming some Island, oft, as Seamen tell,
> With fixed Anchor in his scaly rind
> Moors by his side under the Lee, while Night
> Invests the Sea, and wished Morn delays.

The almost frightening relevance of this simile lies partially in its allusion to Isaiah (27:1): "The Lord . . . shall punish leviathan the piercing serpent, even leviathan, that crooked serpent; and he shall slay the dragon that *is* in the sea." Equally disturbing is our knowledge that in time men will anchor to leviathan, mistaking it for land, just as they shall cling to Satan. It is surely more than coincidental that in Hebrew "leviathan" means "a heap of serpents,"[6] and in the bestiaries the whale is a symbol of Satan.[7] Too, the whale's slumbering on the "*Norway* foam" is almost certainly related to Satan's emergence from the Nor[th]way, just as the "scaly rind" anticipates the serpent's scales which, according to the Book of Job, are the pride of leviathan. "Rind" may also suggest the enticing skin of the fatal fruit, for "it was from out the rind of one apple tasted, that the knowledge of good and evil, as two twins cleaving together, leaped forth into the world."[8]

It is unfortunately also likely that Whaler's method of pictorially representing the similes leads him to stress likeness to the virtual exclusion of heterogeneity. Kingsley Widmer, on the other hand, rightly serves as a corrective, recognizing that disparity is also important.[9] Contrast is intrinsic to *Paradise Lost*. Arguing that the narrator's function is to reveal an innocent world fallen man has never known, Anne Davidson Ferry justly observes that the only way to comprehend an unfallen Eden is to contrast it with the postlapsarian world of everyman's experience.[10] Simile is an excellent device for delineating such contrasts.

Douglas Bush and Kingsley Widmer demonstrate that similes in *Paradise Lost* create not only contrast and distance, but irony as well. In a simile comparing the warring rebel angels to the brave soldiers of antiquity, Bush illustrates ironic contrast. Satan's angels moved (1.550-67)

> In perfect *Phalanx* to the *Dorian* mood
> Of Flutes and soft Recorders; such as rais'd
> To highth of noblest temper Heroes old
> Arming to Battle, and instead of rage
> Deliberate valor breath'd, firm and unmov'd
> With dread of death to flight or foul retreat,
> Nor wanting power to mitigate and swage
> With solemn touches, troubl'd thoughts, and chase
> Anguish and doubt and fear and sorrow and pain
> From mortal or immortal minds. Thus they
> Breathing united force with fixed thought
> Mov'd on in silence to soft Pipes that charm'd
> Thir painful step o'er the burnt soil; and now
> Advanc't in view they stand, a horrid Front
> Of dreadful length and dazzling Arms, in guise
> Of Warriors old with order'd Spear and Shield,
> Awaiting what command thir mighty Chief
> Had to impose.

Although emphasizing the "order, courage, and dignity of the marching angels," Bush points out that Milton also "makes most of the borrowed matter into a simile and implies a contrast between the 'Deliberate valor' of ancient heroes arming for battle in assurance of divine help and the 'rage' that has inspired the defeated and evil host of hell."[11]

The Miltonic simile in *Paradise Lost* is indeed a complex device, whose relevance, while it can no longer be doubted, is perhaps even more pertinent than initially supposed. To read primarily for sameness as Whaler does, or for disparity as Widmer and Bush, is to be false to Milton's vision. In spite of his many brilliant insights, Whaler's quasi-mathematical equations finally do him a disservice because his analyses are so concentrated upon the likeness between terms of a simile that he usually fails to discern differences. Possibly to adjust Whaler's emphasis on homologation, Widmer and Bush go to the other extreme, deemphasizing similarities in their search for ironic disproportion. In *Milton's Grand Style*, however, Christopher Ricks more nearly approaches the proper balance (*P.L.* 1.338-44):

> As when the potent Rod
> Of *Amram's* Son in *Egypt's* evil day
> Wav'd round the Coast, up call'd a pitchy cloud
> Of *Locusts*, warping on the Eastern Wind,
> That o'er the Realm of impious *Pharaoh* hung
> Like Night, and darken'd all the Land of *Nile*:
> So numberless were those bad Angels seen.

"The relevance of the locusts' is obvious," says Ricks,[12]

the evil of Egypt follows the account of 'Busiris and his Memphian Chivalrie' [see 1.307]; and Milton brings out the piety of Moses by stressing the impiety of his adversary. Is it possible then to think that Milton was not making deliberate use, not only of the similarity of Satan and Moses at this point, but also of the hideous differences between them?

Indeed, I believe that the Miltonic simile *is* working in two opposite directions at once.

The misreading of similes has been due, certainly at least in part, to inattention to genre. Requirements for reading an epic such as *Paradise Lost* necessarily differ from those of fiction or drama. Novels and plays are set in time; they possess a definite beginning, middle, and end, but neither the time scheme nor the logic of an epic such as *Paradise Lost* is linear like an Aristotelian syllogism. Epic does not proceed from "if" to "then," nor from *A* to *B* in an ordinary straight line, nor does it proceed from simple present time to future or from past time to present. *Paradise Lost* does not progress like an arrow because, as Isabel MacCaffrey has ably demonstrated, the epic is circular in structure.[13] Following the invocation, the poem opens *in medias res* with the vanquished devils sprawled on the burning marl of hell. Through a series of flashbacks, however, the epic actually begins in paradise, and finishes in the new paradise at the end of time. Just as Virgil's *Aeneid* really commences in Troy and terminates in the new Troy, the movement in *Paradise Lost* from paradise to paradise suggests a circle.

As a circle, paradise speaks of time and eternity. Through the circular action of the poem, time is either made "full" or, since the epic starts and ends in paradise, time becomes timeless. The circular motif is reflected in a structural and thematic circularity: what was lost at the Fall is restored; what has died revives; what has fallen rises; what was winter springs anew. To read epic, then, such ingredients as plot and character development understandably diminish in importance, despite A. J. A. Waldock's arguments to the contrary. Satan, for instance, does not degenerate or disintegrate as he might in a drama—he only becomes *more* obviously satanic as the epic unfolds.[14] Everything is essentially implicit in the beginning of *Paradise Lost*, to be further revealed "by tract of time" (5.498). Such a view of epic is entirely consistent if, as it does, the poem begins and ends in the same place. Only after time has run full circle, however, does it become entirely clear that the paradise lost by Adam and Eve through "Man's First Disobedience" (1.1) has foreshadowed the "paradise within" promised in book 12, as well as the new paradise at the end of time, when all becomes heavenly.

To read both *Paradise Lost* and its similes adequately, therefore, requires a different approach, namely, familiarity with *discordia concors*. In *Areopagitica* Milton makes an analogous statement:[15]

Truth indeed came once into the world . . . and was a perfect shape, [but then mankind] took the virgin Truth, hewed her lovely form into a thousand pieces and scattered them to the four winds, [and] we have not yet found them all, . . . nor ever shall do, till her Master's second coming. He shall bring together every joint and member, and shall mold them into an immortal feature of loveliness and perfection.

In other words, in paradise truth was complete and entire until divided at the Fall. At Christ's Incarnation truth again entered time and the world, from out of eternity, but at the Crucifixion it was shattered once more. Man is thus left until the day of his salvation "searching" for what he knows not, by what he knows, "still closing up truth to truth"[16] as he finds it. This seems to be what Milton achieves through simile in *Paradise Lost*—he searches for truth, searching for what is unknown by what is known, comparing and contrasting, placing one thing next to another in analogy, in order to reconstruct the truth of man's condition. The Miltonic simile is an embodiment of this procedure. Slowly the reader circles in upon the essence of the epic theme of loss and restoration, death and life, until it is clear that the loss *is* restoration; the two seemingly contrary possibilities are linked as one.

To examine *Paradise Lost* through *discordia concors* differs from the approach of critics previously discussed. Their points are important and well taken, but their emphases must be altered, because the Miltonic simile cannot be read *now* for likeness and *then* for difference. Rather, it demands to be read simultaneously for likeness and difference, for discord and for concord. Not only does the simile as a unit invite comparison and contrast with other related portions in the epic, but it equally invites comparison and contrast within itself, because the words and situations concurrently imply their opposites. Simile thus becomes paradoxical.

Since it would be impossible to discuss effectively all the similes in *Paradise Lost*, an extremely close analysis of one simile and its far-reaching ramifications may serve to test these theories.

In book 6 the angel Raphael relates to Adam and Eve the story of the war in heaven that raged for three days and led to the expulsion and ruin of Satan and his rebel clan. On the first day of confrontation Satan appears (6.99-107)

John Milton: Opposites and Multiplicity Resolved

> High in the midst exalted as a God
> Th' Apostate in his Sun-bright Chariot sat
> Idol of Majesty Divine, enclos'd
> With Flaming Cherubim, and golden Shields;
> Then lighted from his gorgeous Throne, for now
> 'Twixt Host and Host but narrow space was left,
> A dreadful interval, and Front to Front
> Presented stood in terrible array
> Of hideous length.

This simile is impressively wrought. Not only is the picture magnificent and sublime in itself, but the language is stately and regal, at every point suggesting that the power and majesty of Satan can and does rival the courts of highest heaven. Emphatically, readers are intended to experience the real and terrifying likeness of Satan to Christ, but simultaneously submerged beneath this awesome panoply of satanic majesty are implications that span the entire epic—for nothing less than the entire epic vision is compressed within this simile.

If the reader keeps *discordia concors* in mind, he is not only forced to compare and contrast within the terms of the analogy, but also to compare and contrast it with other relevant passages. Satan sits "exalted as a God"—so very like to God, but conversely there is an immediate awareness that on the third day Christ is to be truly exalted by God the Father. Satan's exaltation implicitly suggests Christ's. Numerous passages evince the differences between them.

In book 3 God discusses with Christ the ransom necessary to redeem mankind. Unlike Satan, Christ's sacrifice and "Humiliation shall exalt" (3.313). The devil has raised himself through pride, presumption, and disobedience to God, while Christ has been exalted not through pride but through humility. In itself it is a paradoxical gesture: Christ will lower himself for the benefit of mankind, and for this selflessness be raised on high, justly exalted.

Earlier in the epic Satan sits on his ostensibly regal throne in hell (2.5-9):

> Satan exalted sat, by merit rais'd
> To that bad eminence; and from despair
> Thus high uplifted beyond hope, aspires
> Beyond thus high, insatiate to pursue
> Vain War with Heav'n.

But his exaltation is pathetic, since irony sharply undercuts its glory. "By merit rais'd" is counterbalanced by "that bad eminence," while "high uplifted" is lowered by "beyond hope." Aspiration is "insatiate" because it is "vain"—useless and ever-empty. For Satan, "exalted" begins to look a bit dubious and tarnished set beside Christ's exaltation.

Crucial nuances of "exalted" are further elucidated when the angel Michael interprets for Adam and Eve the "mysterious terms" (10.173) of Christ's judgment that the seed of Eve (that is, Christ, born of Mary, "second Eve") shall bruise the head of the serpent, Satan (12.451-58):

> Then to the Heav'n of Heav'ns he [Christ] shall ascend
> With victory, triúmphing through the air
> Over his foes and thine; there shall surprise
> The Serpent, Prince of air, and drag in Chains
> Through all his Realm, and there confounded leave;
> Then enter into glory, and resume
> His Seat at God's right hand, exalted high
> Above all names in Heav'n.

Christ's exaltation is wholly associated with his victory, ascent, and glory. "His Seat at God's right hand" is not deprecated as a "bad eminence" as Satan's was, nor is his exaltation dimmed by hint of pride or vain enterprise.

By comparing and contrasting the various connotations of "exalted" within the text, it now takes on new weight and significance in the test simile. With its accumulated meanings, it may now be more easily seen that Satan, "exalted as a God" has become a paradoxical statement. Contrariety is in simultaneous equipoise with sameness. Even etymologically "exalted" is paradoxical. Derived from the Latin *altus*, meaning "high" or "deep," "exalted" is one of those words that possess at once two antithetical possibilities. What could more appropriately suggest the biblical paradox of Christ's humble exaltation while also describing Satan's proud, vaunting exaltation? In one word, "exalted," is centered the epic action of *Paradise Lost* and implicitly of *Paradise Regained*. The fall of Satan, and with him, mankind, is quietly adumbrated at the same time that Christ's Resurrection and man's is foreshadowed. The Fall is thus linked in paradox to the promised restoration.

John Milton: Opposites and Multiplicity Resolved

Although opposites, they share the same curious relationship as that posited by Heraclitus: "The way up and the way down are one and the same."[17] Paradoxically, both rising and falling serve the greater glory of God, for "Rising or falling still advance his praise" (5.191). Each action, whether good or ill, has its place in the circle of God. Even Satan's evil turns to good in time.

But the phrase "exalted as a God" is only one facet of this simile's complexity. In the second line Satan advances in his "Sun-bright Chariot." The phrase "Sun-bright" contains the familiar Renaissance pun on "sun" and "Son," which is especially appropriate here, for Satan is competing with the Son of God who will appear on the third day of controversy in "The Chariot of Paternal Deity" (6.750). Satan sits in his "Sun-bright Chariot," mere "Idol of Majesty Divine," but Christ is blessed by the Father who "on his Son with Rays direct / Shone full" (6.719-20). The "Sun-bright" apostate will be met by the full-blazing Son "and the Orbs / Of his fierce Chariot" (6.829-30). Before Christ the satanic host will fail: "All courage; down thir idle weapons dropp'd" (6.839), just fate for spirits "Idol of Majesty Divine." Thus these puns, like the words "exalted" and "Idol," which achieved punlike status through repeated contrasts, also anticipate the coming triumph of Christ, while simultaneously hinting at Satan's demise: all that is imperfect in Satan is perfected and made complete in Christ.

Compressing several meanings at once, as he customarily does, Milton puns quite seriously on the implications of "idol" and "idle" in the third line of the test simile. "Idol" may be traced to the Latin *idolum*, but originally its roots were in the Greek εἰδωλον, from εἰδος, meaning "form" or "shape" (*OED*). Primarily, however, "idol" refers to "an image or similitude of a deity or divinity, used as an object of worship," but "idol" also denotes "a sham; a pretender" (*OED*).[18] Satan is equally "idle" of majesty because his efforts are to be, in fact, vain and useless. Moreover, "Idol of Majesty Divine" anticipates the fall of Satan since he is only an eidolon, or representation of deity, and not the true God. The loyal angel

Abdiel is appalled that "such resemblance of the Highest / Should yet remain" (6.114-15). Satan is false—an impostor who pretends to majesty and who would become the Son (sun), and who would be exalted as God. But the puns on "idol" and on "sun" subtly indicate that Satan is riding for a fall, because his presumption is vanity itself. Through such puns the devil's likeness to Christ simultaneously becomes a grotesque parody of godliness—a travesty of deity. The magnificence and grandeur of the stately language ironically delineate not only the proximity but also the vast gulf between the Son and the one who would be Son.

Travesty creates its own ambiance of paradox, because the copy must be compared to the original. By depicting the devil as a mockery of godliness, Milton reminds us of Christ's true godliness. Travesty tacitly reveals its polar opposite, just as puns do. Satan, in his "Sun-bright Chariot," immediately invites comparison and contrast with Christ who will arrive on the third day in his celestial "Chariot of Paternal Deity."

In countless instances Milton exploits the ambiguities of words to mirror the meaning of a paradise lost. An extraordinary example may be seen in his daring use of the word "noon"[19] which in the seventeenth century meant both midday and midnight. Significantly, Milton places nearly all the important events and encounters in *Paradise Lost* at noon—the darkest hour and the brightest hour. Eve eats the forbidden fruit at the evil hour of noon—ostensibly the darkest hour for mankind, but symbolically also the brightest hour, because simultaneously it promises restoration while marking the Fall and loss of paradise. And again, Adam and Eve are expelled from the Garden at the "hour precise" (12.589). At the seemingly dark hour of expulsion, Milton suggests that light and hope are part of the overall pattern of providence. Although the "hour precise" is not precisely stated, Milton implies that it is noon. Ordinarily one might expect that the sinful pair would be ejected from paradise immediately following their fatal error. Darkness seems most appropriate to dismissal, but Milton carefully permits Adam and Eve to spend another entire night in Eden. A new day dawns and light comes into the

John Milton: Opposites and Multiplicity Resolved

world and with it a sense of hope. Only if the "hour precise" is noon, can Milton imply that the darkest hour is full of hope. The exodus at noon pinpoints in paradox the vision that in man's falling is his rising, that the darkest hour *is* the brightest. Here the coincidence of opposites depends upon Milton's interpretation of time and eternity. The Fall is "fortunate" only in the fullness of time, or outside of earthly time and "tenses." The yoking of the two contraries of rising and falling, dark and light, becomes transcendent only when seen within the circle of God, which symbolizes eternity.

Words such as "noon," "exalted," "Sun-bright," and "idol," create a pattern of *discordia concors* throughout the entire epic. With greatest economy Milton yokes light and darkness, rising and falling, loss and restoration, within a single simile. There are, however, difficult problems for the reader. In *Paradise Lost* virtually everything is pictured in opposites; for example, God is "dark with excessive bright" (3.380) and hell is "darkness visible" (1.63). Satan, the Prince of Darkness, similarly appears in the test simile in a radiant, "Sun-bright Chariot." He, too, is dark with excessive bright. The mind longs to simplify this apparent confusion and align Satan very properly with darkness, and Christ with light—to make a choice at every antithetical word, deciding that in one instance Lucifer is Christ, and in the next that he is Satan. But the difficulties with the paradoxical kind of *discordia concors* are further magnified by Milton's repeated hints that heaven and earth are not so very different after all—that everything differs only "in degree" but is "of kind the same" (5.574ff., 468-90).

In the following simile Milton compares the universe to a tree (5.468-90):

> To whom the winged Hierarch [Raphael] repli'd.
> O *Adam*, one Almighty is, from whom
> All things proceed, and up to him return,
> If not deprav'd from good, created all
> Such to perfection, one first matter all,
> Indu'd with various forms, various degrees
> Of substance, and in things that live, of life;
> But more refin'd, more spiritous, and pure,

John Milton: Opposites and Multiplicity Resolved

> As nearer to him plac't or nearer tending
> Each in thir several active Spheres assign'd,
> Till body up to spirit work, in bounds
> Proportion'd to each kind. So from the root
> Springs lighter the green stalk, from thence the leaves
> More aery, last the bright consummate flow'r
> Spirits odorous breathes: flow'rs and thir fruit
> Man's nourishment, by gradual scale sublim'd
> To vital spirits aspire, to animal,
> To intellectual, give both life and sense,
> Fancy and understanding, whence the Soul
> Reason receives, and reason is her being,
> Discursive, or Intuitive; discourse
> Is oftest yours, the latter most is ours,
> Differing but in degree, of kind the same.

Initially Milton presents a monistic view of the universe: all God's creations "proceed" from him, and "up to him return." Although God's handiwork appears in "various forms" and "various degrees / Of substance," everything is ultimately related because each creature shares a portion of God's being. Since the universe in Milton's cosmology was created *ex deo*, "one first matter all," it follows that all matter is continuous and that man is godlike.

But Milton's philosophy is more complicated than simple monism, since next he sets up a platonic hierarchy, placing all matter "in bounds," according to the properties of each. A most curious situation. At first the poet asserts that all matter is continuous—that there are no absolute dichotomies—and then he separates matter "Each in thir several active Spheres assign'd."

The problem is further tangled by the introduction of the simile "So from the root / Springs lighter the green stalk." The universe of the preceding lines is likened to a tree. At the lowest point is the root; ascending upwards are the stalk and leaves; at the highest point are the flowers and fruit. The tree is therefore like the cosmic hierarchy, in which matter is placed "in bounds."

The real difficulty arises when "last the bright consummate flow'r" is reached, because here Milton steps out of "bounds," as it were. Since in the seventeenth century plants were not thought to breathe, it is strange to say that "the bright consummate flow'r / Spirits breathes." "Spirits odorous" obviously refer to the fragrance of the flower, but they might equally refer to man's "spirits," especially as it is he who breathes. Such a reading is reinforced when Milton declares that the flowers and their spirits are "man's nourishment," and that they "by gradual scale sublim'd/To vital spirits aspire." "Aspire" is the same as "breathes," so that the flowers' "spirits" are actually man's. When food is digested or heated, "spirits" are produced, which were believed to bind body and soul, as well as parts of the soul itself. But certainly one had expected that the poet would have distinguished between plants and man. In a platonic system plants would have been completely separated from man—yet Milton deliberately obscures that distinction. He has even gone so far as to *link* plants with mankind through the pun on "spirits."

The implications of this bold attitude are far-reaching. Through puns Milton asserts a monistic world-view ("one first matter all") at the very same time that he asserts a dualistic view, separating matter "in bounds." Punning language thus creates a paradoxical philosophy which suggests that the contrarieties in life are virtually indivisible. Similes therefore ought not be read sequentially for sameness and disparity, nor should they be read simply for likeness to the exclusion of difference, or vice versa. Milton's is primarily a vision of continuity which surpasses a world where labels neatly divide things into simple categories. The simultaneous declaration of monism and dualism is not only analogous to, but a variation of, the poet's more fundamental belief that sameness always coexists with contrariety. Just as the pun on "spirits" joined man with plants, so Christ and Satan, like good and evil in *Areopagitica*, are brought together into meridian correspondence. The conjunction of Christ and Satan as noonday sun in the test simile is made possible because both opposites are depicted in identical imagery and because puns such as "Sun-bright" tend to obscure their polarity. Moreover, Milton has intentionally blurred their separation; he makes it exceedingly difficult to draw the thin line between the terms of a paradox. The great danger of the *discordia concors* in all similes, then, is the failure to recognize the urgency of making those distinctions that do separate opposites yoked together in the fallen world. Like Stanley Fish in *Surprised by Sin*, I also believe that Milton wants readers to feel guilty—that we are like Adam and Eve, and therefore subject to the same illusions. When Milton describes Satan and Christ in identical imagery, he permits us to confront the same moral choices as our first parents. If in our reading we too are "by some fair appearing good surpris'd" (9.354), then we share the Fall. But once our fault is recognized, we see that hope still remains, if we read aright. And to do that requires knowledge of *discordia concors*.

Although submerged in the test simile, difference and diversity, to the point of contrariety, prevent the resolution of Satan into identity and equivalence with Christ. This is why Whaler's "equations" are so deceptive. Difference and contrariety cannot be easily accounted for in diagrams that are conceptually linear and in simple one-to-one relationships. In the test simile Milton is using one word, "sun" (or "exalted," "idol," etc.), for two opposite things. Although deliberately created in the same imagery of dark brightness, the relationship between Satan and Christ remains paradoxical. Christ is not Satan nor is Satan Christ; they are diametrically opposed. Simile also retains its paradoxical nature—it is likeness at the same time that it is difference. In *Religio Medici* (2.2) Sir Thomas Browne observes:

Nor doth the similitude of creatures disparage the variety of nature, nor any way confound the workes of God. For even in things alike, there is diversitie, and those that doe seeme to accord, doe manifestly disagree. And thus is Man like God, for in the same things that wee resemble him, wee are utterly different from him. There was never anything so like another, as in all points to concurre, there will ever some reserved difference slip in, to prevent the Identity, without which, two severall things would not be alike, but the same, which is impossible.

Difference must therefore be searched out to prevent likeness from collapsing into sameness.

To magnify the incongruities in similes, Satan in his "Sun-bright Chariot" must be contrasted with other portions of the epic. When, for instance, he flies from hell in search of paradise, "The golden Sun in splendor likest Heaven / Allur'd his eye" (3.572-73). So irresistibly is the devil attracted, that one is again reminded that he desires to become the sun as Son. Landing on the sun (3.591-92), Satan in his baseness is contrasted with the sun's purity which gleams "beyond expression bright, / Compar'd with aught on Earth, Metal or Stone" (3.606-12):

> What wonder then if fields and regions here
> Breathe forth *Elixir* pure, and Rivers run
> Potable Gold, when with one virtuous touch
> Th' Arch-chemic Sun so far from us remote
> Produces with Terrestrial Humor mixt
> Here in the dark so many precious things
> Of color glorious and effect so rare?

The alchemical imagery particularly underscores the essential purity and hence moral value of the celestial body. The contrast between Satan's wickedness and the sun's goodness is made explicit when Uriel, the angel who represents God's "eyes / That run through all the Heav'ns, or down to th' Earth" (3.650-51), finds himself accosted by the fiend, that "Spirit impure" (3.630).

Moreover, the flame that lights Satan's being is "inflam'd with rage" (4.9) because inwardly a "hot Hell . . . always in him burns" (9.467). His hatred for the sun is symbolic of the wrath directed against the Son of God (4.32-41):

> O thou that with surpassing Glory crown'd,
> Look'st from thy sole Dominion like the God
> Of this new World; at whose sight all the Stars
> Hide thir diminisht heads; to thee I call,
> But with no friendly voice, and add thy name
> O Sun, to tell thee how I hate thy beams
> That bring to my remembrance from what state
> I fell, how glorious once above thy Sphere;
> Till Pride and worse Ambition threw me down
> Warring in Heav'n against Heav'n's matchless King.

The sun's brilliance and purity testify to the former glory of Satan, while simultaneously preparing the reader for the test simile in which the devil is yet glorious. This passage and others help to differentiate the satanic sun, Uriel's sun, and God's Son, so that when we return to Satan in his "Sun-bright Chariot" differences are already apparent—differences that prevent the simile from being read primarily for likeness. It is then possible to form expectations that, like the stars, Satan will also eventually "hide" his "diminisht" head, with his "lustre visibly impair'd" (4.850), and his "splendor" "faded . . . wan" (4.870).

From the very beginning of *Paradise Lost* there is latent anticipation that Satan's glory will be diminished by the full-blazing radiance of God's Son. The devil's aspect (1.591-600)

> had yet not lost
> All her Original brightness, nor appear'd
> Less than Arch-Angel ruin'd, and th' excess
> Of Glory obscur'd: As when the Sun new ris'n
> Looks through the Horizontal misty Air
> Shorn of his Beams, or from behind the Moon
> In dim Eclipse disastrous twilight sheds
> On half the Nations, and with fear of change
> Perplexes Monarchs. Dark'n'd so, yet shone
> Above them all th' Arch-Angel.

As the sun in cloud and in eclipse, the apostate conveys the sense of "Glory obscur'd"—of a light that will gradually be extinguished into the total darkness of full eclipse. The satanic sun in mist and eclipse is in polar contradistinction to the Almighty who on his Son (10.65-67)

> Blaz'd forth unclouded Deity; he full
> Resplendent all his Father manifest
> Express'd.

The "excess" of Satan's "glory" is reduced—"obscur'd" in mist, but the radiance of the true sun (Son), "That glorious Form, that Light unsufferable" ("Nativity Ode" 8) is simultaneously magnified. By contrast, the true Son implicitly burns the brighter and his triumph looms the more imminent.

This simile not only quite literally adumbrates the fall of Satan, but it also anticipates, as Cleanth Brooks has shown, the dark satanic twilight that shall soon cover the earth, enveloping both Adam and Eve, and "half the Nations." It is indeed a "disastrous twilight" in the etymological sense of "disastrous," which is derived from the Latin *dis* + *astrum*, meaning "evil star."[20] At Eve's fall the darkness of Satan's malignity will blight the earth. The "fear of change" that "perplexes Monarchs" is well founded, for the Fall is reflected by cruel change on earth. The course of Christ as sun (Son) is diverted: God punishes man by teaching "the fixt [stars] / Thir influence malignant when to show'r" (10.661-62) on earth. And (10.412-14)

> the blasted Stars lookt wan,
> And Planets, Planet-strook, real Eclipse
> Then suffer'd.

Meanwhile "grateful vicissitude" (6.8) turns to winter wind and bitter sky.

The eclipse simile foreshadows the time when the devil will be "shorn of his Beams," eclipsed by the true Son, Jesus Christ; but it also suggests the fate of Adam and Eve. Like Herculean Samson, who lost his strength at the cutting edge of Delilah's shears, our first parents shall in time lose their strength, their virtue, through Satan (9.1059-63):[21]

> So rose the *Danite* strong
> *Herculean Samson* from the Harlot-lap
> Of *Philistean Dalilah*, and wak'd
> Shorn of his strength, They [Adam, Eve] destitute
>   and bare
> Of all thir virtue.

Adam and Eve will suffer the inclemency of nature, but their loss of virtue also burdens them. With Satan's eclipse, follows man's. Christ's final victory, however, returns man to original brightness, while Satan is cast into utter obscurity.

Satanic splendor is further qualified when news spreads of man's entry into sin. On the devil's hellish throne (10.447-52)

> Down a while
> He sat, and round about him saw unseen:
> At last as from a Cloud his fulgent head
> And shape Star-bright appear'd, or brighter, clad
> With what permissive glory since his fall
> Was left him, or false glitter.

Satan's glory is only so much as God's greater glory permits, which further distinguishes the essential contrariety between Christ and the apostate who is "idol of Majesty Divine." Satan's "false glitter" reinforces the pun on "idol," because not only is his superficial radiance diminished by comparison with heavenly glory, but as a "false glitter" it also mirrors his internal deceit and drossy impurity. "Since his fall" Satan *is* "false," and can now be more easily seen for what he is: a similacrum of "Majesty Divine," composed entirely of counterfeit glitter. Myriad examples of the sun's and the Son's purity and unclouded brilliance now come rushing back to widen the contrast. The true Son is (7.194-96):

> Girt with Omnipotence, with Radiance crown'd
> Of Majesty Divine, Sapience and Love
> Immense, and all his Father in him shone.

Further density in the original test simile may be detected by additional comparison and contrast. Intermediate to Christ's arrival on the third day of battle in heaven, the archangel Michael confronts Satan (6.301-06):

> for likest Gods they seem'd,
> Stood they or mov'd, in stature, motion, arms
> Fit to decide the Empire of great Heav'n.
> Now wav'd thir fiery Swords, and in the Air
> Made horrid Circles; two broad Suns thir Shields
> Blaz'd opposite.

Fierce swords slash the air in "horrid Circles"—a shape repeated in the round shields that "blaz'd opposite" like "two broad Suns." Miltón states the situation precisely. Both Michael and Satan appear "likest Gods," but not only are they physically opposed as suns, they are also morally opposite. The image of the circle, so important in *Paradise Lost*, is fulfilled with the advent of Christ, the Son who blazes "forth unclouded Deity." As his loyal servant, Michael is in effect a vice-regent sun. His contest with Satan is emblematic of the approaching encounter between Christ the Son, and the "Sunbright" apostate. In his description of the battle, Raphael further reveals the nature of similes (6.310-15):

> such as, to set forth
> Great things by small, if Nature's concord broke,
> Among the Constellations war were sprung,
> Two Planets rushing from aspect malign
> Of fiercest opposition in mid Sky,
> Should combat, and thir jarring Spheres confound.

John Milton: Opposites and Multiplicity Resolved

In mid-sky two suns, Michael and Satan, clash in a combat that not only symbolically anticipates Christ's eventual victory and Satan's defeat, but also focuses attention on the temporal and spatial aspect of Milton's similes. Michael and Satan meet in mid-heaven as two broadly shining suns. Like the rebellious angels who lay prostrate in hell for "Nine times the Space that measures Day and Night" (1.50), space here also suggests time. Since the sun is most broad at noon, Milton supplies secondary hints that pinpoint significant action at high noon. The test simile even states that Satan sat "High in the midst exalted as a God": the midpoint in space is the midpoint in time. Noon is implicitly the imaginative time of the similes. Michael's confrontation intimates that Satan will fight again on the next day in mid-heaven as "sun" meets Son at noon. This simile is thus a focal point in time and space between dark and light, up and down, loss and restoration, death and life. It is the carefully contrived, perfect coincidence of opposites.

Instead of similes drawing together things of equal magnitude and emphasizing their likeness to the point of identity, Milton purposely sets "forth / Great things by small." The movement toward identity is accomplished rather by comparing one thing with its polar opposite: the great and small, good and evil, dark and light, Christ and Satan. Through *discordia concors* Milton fuses "great" and "small" into the unit of the simile, thereby creating the paradoxical effects so characteristic of *Paradise Lost*. In the test simile, for example, the "sun" is both Satan and Christ, the meanest and the greatest. Knowledge of *discordia concors* permits readers themselves to set forth great next to small so that the accumulated connotations of the language reveal how contrariety is simultaneously juxtaposed with similarity in the Miltonic simile.

On the third day of discord in heaven, Christ the true sun rushes forth in the "Chariot of Paternal Deity" to meet Satan in his "Sun-bright Chariot." Heaven's chariot appears (6. 751-56),

John Milton: Opposites and Multiplicity Resolved

> Flashing thick flames, Wheel within Wheel, undrawn,
> Itself instinct with Spirit, but convoy'd
> By four Cherubic shapes, four Faces each
> Had wondrous, as with Stars thir bodies all
> And Wings were set with Eyes, with Eyes the Wheels
> Of Beryl, and careering Fires between.

The "Flaming Cherubim, and golden Shields" accompanying Satan's chariot inevitably invite contrast with Christ's "four Cherubic shapes." "Wheel within Wheel, undrawn" but spiritually moved, the heavenly chariot varies markedly from its satanic counterpart, which is impelled by presumption, vanity, and disobedience. "From the living Wheels" Christ shoots "forth pernicious fire" among the satanic host (6.846, 849), who fall "exhausted, spiritless, afflicted" (6.852), "wither'd [of] all thir strength, / And of thir wonted vigor . . . drain'd" (6.850-51).

Having ejected Satan and the rebellious host from heaven, Christ victoriously rejoins his Father (6.889-92):

> Triumphant through mid Heav'n, into the Courts
> And Temple of his mighty Father Thron'd
> On high; who into Glory him receiv'd,
> Where now he sits at the right hand of bliss.

Now even the "gorgeous Throne" on which the apostate sits in our test simile is put into umbrage, darkened through comparison and contrast with the throne of God. There has been no portion of the test simile which has not yielded to qualification when compared to other passages.

Returning to the simile after numerous efforts to adjust the tendency to read either for similarity or dissimilarity, it is now impossible to regard Satan as simply sitting "High in the midst, exalted as a God" in his "Sun-bright Chariot." What might initially appear as almost prosaic resemblances are now charged with powerful contrasts. The meaning and nature of the Miltonic simile is always contingent upon bringing the submerged *discordia concors* to the surface. Only then does the subtly compressed simile reveal how difference and contrariety are simultaneously implied while likeness is asserted.

Since *Paradise Lost* is a Christian epic, the paradox of *discordia concors* is eminently suited to portray not only the traditional paradoxes of Christianity, but also Milton's vision of man's fallen "double . . . Mind" ("The Mower against Gardens" 9). As the lowest common denominator of the poem, the paradoxical quality of *discordia concors* reflects the mind in a way that prose cannot. The fatal change within the mind after the Fall was subsequently detected in language.[22] Sin orders Death to wreak havoc on man (10.605-08):

> whatever thing
> The Scythe of Time mows down, devour unspar'd,
> Till I in Man residing through the Race,
> His thoughts, his looks, words, actions all infect.

The paradox possible in poetic language has been, perhaps, the only way to imitate the flawed quality of postlapsarian life.

Discordia concors is, I believe, the complicated language of the mind—even of dreams and the unconscious. "Every element in a dream can," writes Sigmund Freud in *The Interpretation of Dreams*, "stand for its opposite just as easily as for itself."[23] Like the mechanism of *discordia concors*, dreams "show a particular preference for combining contraries into a unity or for representing them as one and the same thing." Moreover, Freud pinpoints similitude as "very highly favored by the mechanism of dream-formation." The simile thus reflects mental activity itself.

Although separated in time, Freud and Milton were both exploring the characteristic operations of the mind, which have not changed very much, if at all. What Freud discovered about the mind through his work with dreams, Milton had also observed in human nature, as the following passage from *Areopagitica* reveals. Milton's reason for choosing the *discordia concors* of simile as his underlying narrative motif becomes clear:[24]

Good and evil we know in the field of this world grow up together almost inseparably; and the knowledge of good is so involved and interwoven with the knowledge of evil, and in so many cunning resemblances hardly to be discerned. . . . It was from out the rind of one apple tasted, that the knowledge of good and evil, as two twins cleaving together, leaped forth into the world. And perhaps this is that doom which Adam fell into of knowing good and evil, that is to say, of knowing good by evil.

Human knowledge and its reflection in language is thus relative; one thing is understood and expressed by comparison with its contrary. Good and evil, like so many other commonly paired opposites—nature and grace, art and nature, black and white, Christ and Satan, seemingly so disparate—are finally not to be wrenched apart, so "involved and interwoven" are they. The fine line between opposites simply cannot be drawn. They, too, "cleave"—in both senses of the word—they come together while they separate, like "brotherly dissimilitudes."[25] Readers cannot clutch one meaning while ignoring its other half. To read exclusively for similarity or solely for disparity is to forget that they are "as two twins cleaving together" within the Miltonic simile.

The double view that the *discordia concors* of similes affords is nothing less than that of the entire epic theme of loss and restoration, death and life, announced in the opening lines of *Paradise Lost* (1.1-6):

> Of Man's First Disobedience, and the Fruit
> Of that Forbidden Tree, whose mortal taste
> Brought Death into the World, and all our woe,
> With loss of *Eden*, till one greater Man
> Restore us, and regain the blissful Seat,
> Sing Heav'nly Muse.

Just as the similes mimetically imitate the epic theme, so the theme of man's falling and rising imitates the poem's circular structure.

If, as they do, similes reflect an implicitly circular theme and poetic structure, then the *discordia concors* or similes which initially appeared to be a yoking of opposites, must now be integrated within the second major kind of *discordia concors*, unity in multiplicity, in which the many gradations between opposites are harmoniously reconciled. In the transcendent version of unity in multiplicity that Milton uses, all the paradoxes of similes are resolved within the providential circle of God, wherein evil turns to good in the fullness of time. "O goodness infinite, goodness immense!" cries Adam when he understands "That all this good of evil shall produce, / And evil turn to good" (12.469-71). In the circle of

John Milton: Opposites and Multiplicity Resolved

rising and falling, the Miltonic simile contains its inherent paradox, the greater one of a paradise lost but recovered "within thee, happier far" (12.587). This extraordinary compression of theme and structure has been revealed in the test simile. To choose but one example, the ambiguity of the word "Sun-bright" expresses the entire epic action, anticipating, as it does, the fall of Satan as well as the triumphal ascent of Christ. Even the movements of Satan and Christ as suns parallel the circuit of the natural sun in the heavens. For instance, Satan is the sun "new ris'n" in the eclipse simile, and Christ, the "mild Judge and Intercessor both" (10.96), comes to judge the errant pair in the cool of the afternoon while "the Sun [descends] in Western cadence low" (10.92). But whether rising or setting suns, the contrarious nature and movements of both Satan and Christ as "sun" (especially in the test simile) are finally resolved in the overall circular pattern of *discordia concors* as unity in multiplicity that first, last, and midst glorifies God.

The all-encircling and all-important Christianized pattern of *discordia concors* as unity in multiplicity is perhaps best exemplified by the Morning Orisons, in which Adam and Eve invite all creation to raise its "various" (5.146) voice in praise of God and his beneficence (5.164-97):

> On Earth join all ye Creatures to extol
> Him first, him last, him midst, and without end.
> Fairest of Stars [Venus-Lucifer], last in the
>   train of Night,
> If better thou belong not to the dawn,
> Sure pledge of day, that crown'st the smiling Morn
> With thy bright Circlet, praise him in thy Sphere
> While day arises, that sweet hour of Prime.
> Thou Sun, of this great World both Eye and Soul,
> Acknowledge him thy Greater, sound his praise
> In thy eternal course, both when thou climb'st,
> And when high Noon hast gain'd, and when thou fall'st.
> Moon, that now meet'st the orient Sun, now fli'st
> With the fixt Stars, fixt in thir Orb that flies,
> And yee five other wand'ring Fires that move
> In mystic Dance not without Song, resound
> His praise, who out of Darkness call'd up Light.
> Air, and ye Elements the eldest birth
> Of Nature's Womb, that in quaternion run
> Perpetual Circle, multiform, and mix

121

> And nourish all things, let your ceaseless change
> Vary to our great Maker still new praise.
> Ye Mists and Exhalations that now rise
> From Hill or steaming Lake, dusky or grey,
> Till the Sun paint your fleecy skirts with Gold,
> In honor to the World's great Author rise,
> Whether to deck with Clouds th' uncolor'd sky,
> Or wet the thirsty Earth with falling showers,
> Rising or falling still advance his praise.
> His praise ye Winds, that from four Quarters blow,
> With every Plant, in sign of Worship wave.
> Fountains and yee, that warble, as ye flow,
> Melodious murmurs, warbling tune his praise.
> Join voices all ye living Souls.

Everything in creation moves within the figure of a Christianized Pythagorean tetrad—the four elements, four seasons, four humours "that in quaternion run / Perpetual Circle." The apparent discords of the universe are concordantly harmonized by the "ceaseless change" of one form turning into its opposite. Falling turns to rising, night to day, down to up reascends in continual revolution.

The "fairest of Stars" is Venus, often called Lucifer, the light-bearer. Lucifer may of course be either Satan, "last in the train of Night," or Christ, the morning star, "sure pledge of day." From yet another point of view, as Prince of Darkness Satan is also the "sure pledge of day," because in time all evil turns to good. As both Satan *and* Christ, Lucifer is analogous to the simile in which the devil rides "exalted as a God / . . . in his Sun-bright Chariot."

Prefiguring Christ's ultimate supremacy, Satan testifies to his own fate, the eventual turning of his evil into goodness and mercy, but his is an unwitting role in the circle of God that first, last, and midst glorifies the Creator. Thus, in Satan's fall Christ's exaltation may be anticipated; in Satan's darkness, Christ's great light; in Adam's fall, his resurrection through God's abundant grace. The Morning Orisons are themselves *Paradise Lost* in epitome, because "in various style" they imitate the epic theme of loss and restoration, of fall and salvation, of death and life. By rising and falling, the narrator himself reflects the circular structure of the poem (3.15-20):

> while in my flight
> Through utter and through middle darkness borne
> With other notes than to th' *Orphean* Lyre
> I sung of *Chaos* and *Eternal Night*,
> Taught by the heav'nly Muse to venture down
> The dark descent, and up to reascend.

Blinded, the narrator flies with inner sight to view the width and breadth of heaven and hell and all that lies between them. As blind but blessed bard, he sings in "harmonious numbers" (3.38) the epic vision of man's first disobedience and the fruit of that forbidden tree. Shaped in poetic number, weight, and measure, the epic theme reflects the composition of the world, which the concept of *discordia concors* itself mirrors.

In 1667 when the first edition of *Paradise Lost* appeared, the poem was divided into ten books, a division that Arthur E. Barker compares with the five-act drama.[26] As a dramatic poem, the Fall becomes the climax of a tragedy. Subsequent action descends to the dark night of earthly life and its bitter reward of death. Dramatic time is linear and incremental; time is duration. In the drama there is a profound sense of the ending as *the* end. In 1674 Milton replaced the assumptions of drama with a different vision. For the second edition of *Paradise Lost* he made slight alterations in the number of lines, but more significantly, he divided two books to create a new pattern of twelve books. The changes are slight in terms of additional lines, but the difference is vast, because it reflects an entirely new perspective. Gone is the model of the five-act drama; it is exchanged for the twelve-book pattern of such classical epics as the *Aeneid*.

Twelve books may be subdivided into four groups of three books each, a system that imitates a Christianized version of the Horatian tetrad. It will be recalled that the Horatian *discordia concors* represents a "jarring harmony" persisting throughout the universe. This uneasy entente was best observed in the four seasons that vary within the confines of the circular year. Thus, the tetrad of *discordia concors* was considered the irreducible design of the cosmos. In four groups of three, the twelve books of *Paradise Lost* parallel Horace's circling year, wherein Satan and Christ "run" in "perpetual Circle," yoked together by *discordia concors*. Unlike the five-act drama that runs downwards in time, the epic revolves in ceaseless circuit. Going in circles implies that the *discordia concors* exemplified by Satan and Christ in the test simile is a continual, repetitious act, shared in every age by every man. Simultaneously the "perpetual Circle" testifies to God's role in converting evil to goodness. The circle thus bears witness to, and is emblematic of, God's eternal ways.

Imitating the art of God, who with golden compasses circumscribed all nature at the creation, Milton has similarly drawn in "various" art the "various" world of nature and of human nature, within his own "perpetual Circle" of twelve books that, like the theme of man's fall and rising, move (5.619-27)

> In song and dance about the sacred Hill,
> Mystical dance, which yonder starry Sphere
> Of Planets and of fixt in all her Wheels
> Resembles nearest, mazes intricate,
> Eccentric, intervolv'd, yet regular
> Then most, when most irregular they seem:
> And in thir motions harmony Divine
> So smooths her charming tones, that God's own ear
> Listens delighted.

In this "various style" (5.146) Milton has praised God and reflected the pattern that God has foretold—that in time evil and discord eventually become goodness and concord. Thus it is that the *discordia concors* of the Miltonic simile, so antithetical and so paradoxical, must finally be seen from the point of view of eternity. From that perspective the yoking of opposites in similes must be integrated within the larger, all-encompassing vision of *discordia concors* that the Morning Orisons exemplify. Only by fitting similes within the greater, transcendent pattern of *discordia concors* as unity in multiplicity, has it become clear how the Fall *is* fortunate.

SEVEN

THE DECLINE

The metaphysical poets of the seventeenth century inherited a rich tradition in *discordia concors*, distinguished by two major patterns. The first is a yoking of opposites, the second, a unity in multiplicity. Each of these patterns appears in two species. Yoking of opposites presents the tension characterized by the bow of Heraclitus, in which contraries are locked in perpetual strife. In its other form, contraries are yoked in order to transcend earthly discord. Similarly, *discordia concors* as unity in multiplicity appears in two species: a Christianized version, whose aim is ultimately to merge with the oneness of God, and a classical, in which earthly disorder is gently blended into harmony. The metaphysicals used the first three of the four varieties; the classical, Horatian version does not reemerge until the later seventeenth and eighteenth centuries, when transcendence is no longer vigorously sought.

Well before the seventeenth century *discordia concors* as unity in multiplicity had generated a corresponding literary style. But it is the pattern of a yoking of opposites that dominates in metaphysical verse. At times, especially in secular lyrics, the yoking suggests the Heraclitean model of perpetual tension, but the most important contribution of the metaphysicals was their development in devotional poetry of a new style whose aim was to resolve those tensions by mentally leaping beyond earth to heaven. As an informing principle within the metaphysical style, the concept of *discordia concors* provides a unique prism with which to distinguish the wit of various metaphysical writers. These distinctions reveal, moreover, that metaphysical wit was not a static phenomenon in the seventeenth century, but an evolving one.

John Donne illustrates the earliest phase of *discordia concors* in the metaphysical era. Despite their great variety, the *Songs and Sonnets* as a collection display Donne's absorption with the nature of emotion, and of human love in particular. In an essay on "The Canonization," Cleanth Brooks precisely characterizes the poetic power underlying Donne's projection of love's ambivalent moods: "If the poet is to be true to his poetry, he must call it neither two nor one; the paradox is his only solution."[1] As a motif, the paradoxical form of *discordia concors* is ideally suited to poetry, for it is both two and one simultaneously. Bringing opposites together in the strained and uncertain harmony of *discordia concors* best reveals the curious cross-currents of human love. In his religious verse, however, Donne also employs a yoking of opposites, but the tortured effort to translate the earthly into the spiritual and heavenly in the *Anniversaries* and *Divine Poems* is so difficult and transcendence so rarely achieved that *discordia concors* here dramatizes the very difficulty of yoking together "the most heterogeneous ideas."

Rather than violently link heterogeneous ideas in Donnean argument, George Herbert dissolves contrariety by discovering "occult resemblances" between his own life and that of Scripture. Biblical metaphors "answer" and dissolve the discord of man's condition; inability to find those "occult resemblances" engenders a profound melancholy in the poet, while sudden revelation of congruity between opposites creates Herbert's typically joyful closures. Because Herbert gently dissolves contrariety in increasingly dense language, without the added freight of a Donnean quasi-logical superstructure, I consider the wit of *The Temple* as transitional between Donne and the later metaphysicals.

Henry Vaughan and Andrew Marvell both represent a later development of *discordia concors*. Vaughan, too, refrains from building an elaborate logical strategy to persuade the reader of a paradoxical truth. His paradoxes, unlike Donne's, are flatly stated and are usually quite traditional. Although sharing Donne's yoking of opposites and Herbert's allusiveness, the creation of Vaughan's paradoxes, such as seeing the sun at midnight, represents a further evolution of *discordia concors*: the first stage for Vaughan involved the discovery of discord amidst apparent concord, a revelation which permitted the second stage of *discordia concors* to occur—the creation of regenerate paradox by yoking together what appears opposite to the external world of appearance. But Vaughan's practice can be described neither in terms of Donne's difficulty in yoking "the most heterogeneous ideas" nor of Herbert's dissolving contrariety in a "discovery of occult resemblances in things apparently unlike." All has become allusively and easily enigmatic in *Silex Scintillans*, because there the logic controlling the paradoxical substructure is largely hidden.

Marvell's poetry perhaps reflects the most complex and eclectic development of *discordia concors* in the period. On the one hand, Marvell extends Herbert's and Vaughan's allusive use of metaphor; on the other, he retains an occasional reminiscence of Donnean logic. But Marvell differs from the other metaphysicals in that the strong polarity marking individual lyrics eventually leads to resolution by *discordia concors* as unity in multiplicity. Considered singly, the ambivalent pattern emergent from Marvell's secular lyrics mirrors the mixed emotions of this world, and also the poet's inability to restore the integrity, the wholeness and purity of the golden era before the Fall. A yoking of opposites like the bow of Heraclitus is particularly suited to reflect the paradoxical world born of the Fall; but such a yoking cannot resolve that tension. For Marvell to resolve this disorder requires desperate doings; nothing less than annihilation and dissolution into the circuit of the "Almighty Sun" suffices. Marvell's return to the older pattern of the circle of God foreshadows the return of unity in multiplicity in which the discords of the four opposing seasons are reconciled within the circle of the harmonious year. As a symbol of time and eternity the circle takes on especially great significance in Marvell, for time hangs heavy until paradise is ready for man to reenter. The end of time seems far in the future, and indeed, time is not to be forced into a new mold or hastened, but rather to be accepted. The "fragrant Zodiack" of the "industrious Bee" is emblematic of man's acceptance of time with the hope of eternity. Instead of an ecstatic apprehension of eternity through the distorted violence of yoking "the most heterogeneous ideas," one feels the poet's gentle contentment, after much struggle, that all turns to honey in heaven's "due season."

For John Milton, even more than for Marvell, the circle is an overarching structural device in *Paradise Lost*, because it contains within itself the epic theme of loss and restoration announced in the opening lines (1.1-5):

> Of Man's First Disobedience, and the Fruit
> Of that Forbidden Tree, whose mortal taste
> Brought Death into the World, and all our woe,
> With loss of *Eden*, till one greater Man
> Restore us, and regain the blissful Seat . . .

Rising or falling, all events—from the Fall of angels and men to man's ultimate rising—move to the greater glory of God, who turns all discord to concord when the circuit of time is complete. The violent yoking of opposites in the Satan-Christ sun simile brings rising and falling together "in the field of this world," but this too must finally be seen within the all-encompassing pattern of circling time. Although anticipated by Marvell in "On a Drop of Dew," *discordia concors* as unity in multiplicity becomes the structural plan of Milton's entire epic. The yoking of opposites, so well exemplified by the Miltonic simile, achieves transcendent meaning only when viewed figurally, within the orb of Christian time, which transmutes all discord into concord; Empedoclean Love has become God's guiding love.

Unlike the earlier metaphysical writers, Milton has minimized the distance and difference between earth and heaven, and in this respect he is quite modern (5.574-76):

> though what if Earth
> Be but the shadow of Heav'n, and things therein
> Each to other like, more than on Earth is thought?

In this view the earth becomes heavenly. For the late eighteenth century especially, however, transcendence is no longer possible because earth has become either too heavenly or too unlike heaven. With the close of the seventeenth century, *discordia concors* as unity in multiplicity becomes a proper ethic for the very mundane, religious, and political affairs of state and commerce, as Wasserman's analyses of Denham's "Cooper's Hill" and Pope's "Windsor Forest" have revealed.[2]

In "Windsor Forest" the classical, nontranscendent form of *discordia concors* as unity in multiplicity reemerges. In this Horatian pattern, it will be recalled, earthly discords are gradually blended and harmonized within the circle of the year. The purpose of this variation is not to leap from earth to heaven but an attempt to illustrate the mechanism of nature. Wasserman argues that the Thames which flows through Windsor Forest is symbolical of England and her role as a nation whose proper pursuit is the peaceful "chace" of commerce, rather than the reckless hunt of war. It is thus in the give and take of trade that England conforms to nature's pattern of *discordia concors* as unity in multiplicity (Wasserman, p. 164):

England's fleets will sail from the Thames to the four ends of the earth; and reciprocally, distant peoples and their goods will cross the joining oceans to sail the Thames: "Whole Nations enter with each swelling Tyde,/. . . Earth's distant End our Glory shall behold, / And the new World launch forth to seek the Old" ("Windsor Forest" 397-404).

The Decline

It seems extraordinary that after so many centuries *discordia concors* should be now embodied as a mercantile doctrine, in the balanced rivalry of nations competing in trade. That the concept should be debased to the coin of merchants is perhaps as great a clue to its ultimate depreciation as one is likely to find. But from another point of view, I believe "Windsor Forest" continues tendencies already present at the turn of the 1600s. Bacon's *New Atlantis*, for instance, may be interpreted as a plea for man's creation of "Bensalem," an earthly paradise, constructed on the basis of knowledge derived from scientific achievements. What was disordered at the Fall can be repaired, Bacon contends, by mankind and machines. One need not inquire into God's ways, or first causes. Since, however, secondary causes are available for careful scrutiny, they ought to be analyzed and changed, if necessary, for the betterment of humanity. Such a philosophy increasingly led to an emphasis on amelioration and progress in time, as opposed to fulfillment in eternity. The notion of time as an arrow of progress, aimed outwards at infinity, did much to cripple the concept of *discordia concors* as a medium of transcendence.

The decline of its importance is due in large measure to the denigration of publicly accepted patterns of cosmic order. *Discordia concors* was, in my opinion, a last impassioned effort either to restore a tenuous concord between opposites or to ease the soul's strife in a temporary vision of heaven. In the eighteenth century standards of social decorum replace cosmic systems of order, and in the nineteenth century universal meaning becomes entirely subjective, relative to a solitary man's perceptions and particular experiences. When the public shared a common vocabulary of cosmic symbols and philosophic principles, including *discordia concors*, a poet was able to mold language in such a way that it reflected those patterns. When the poet touched one string, the whole of humanity might respond in the same chord. But when such organizing concepts and symbols disappeared entirely, little remained but bare language itself.³ Thus by the close of the eighteenth century, and to this day, the poetic act is creative not only of the poem, but of the poem as a cosmic structure—it is the work of the romantic imagination responding to nature's sublimity; God no longer raises the metaphysical poet's wit to create metaphors that mirror divine order underlying the universe.

The growing acceptance during the seventeenth and eighteenth centuries of the scientific world-view proposed earlier by Sir Francis Bacon and his followers did much to diminish the effectiveness of *discordia concors* as the informing element of metaphysical wit. Bacon deplores what Milton perceives as the natural condition of the world and of man's mind. In *Areopagitica* Milton asserts: "Good and evil we know in the field of this world grow up together almost inseparably; and the knowledge of good is so involved and interwoven with the knowledge of evil, and in so many cunning resemblances hardly to be discerned,"⁴ that it is virtually impossible to separate them. Using similar language, but with radically different implications, Bacon states in the preface to the *Magna Instauratio*:⁵

The universe to the eye of the human understanding is framed like a labyrinth, presenting as it does on every side so many ambiguities of way, such deceitful resemblances of objects and signs, natures so irregular in their lines and so knotted and entangled.

Bacon is impatient with the very ambiguities and complexities that Milton and the other metaphysical poets discern as the nature of truth. Bacon wishes to sweep away the cobwebs of so much detrimental cogitation that leads only to error. Originally the mind was thought to mirror the universe and language mirrored the mind, but Bacon believed that wit hinders an understanding of the world. Thus, wit might no longer discover or forge "occult resemblances" within the universe—"the understanding," dictates Bacon, "must not . . . be allowed to jump and fly from particulars to remote axioms."⁶ To apprehend truth, as the metaphysical writers did, by yoking together "the most heterogeneous ideas" becomes impossible in such a restricted atmosphere: "The understanding," says Bacon, "must not . . . be supplied with wings, but rather hung with weights to keep it from leaping and flying."[7]

In the early 1600s Ben Jonson proclaimed with heartfelt sincerity in *Timber; or, Discoveries* that "Poesy" is the "Queene of Arts: which had her Originall from heaven."[8] Because earth then to some extent reflected heaven, the rewards of studying poetry were many, but chiefly this: it "offers to mankinde a certaine rule, and Patterne of living well, and happily." At the close of the seventeenth century no longer might an Elizabeth Drury "for life, and death a patterne bee" as she had in *The Second Anniversary* (524), for the pattern that the wit of *discordia concors* created had steadily disappeared. When Dryden wrote the "Ode to Mrs Anne Killigrew," he praised the young girl in such fashion as to invite comparison with Elizabeth Drury, but Anne's death, although elegantly memorialized, does not poetically become an example for the living as Elizabeth's did. Dryden's emphasis is not the poet's and reader's ecstatic apprehension through *discordia concors* of a reordered earth as a mirror of heaven, but rather, an expressed desire that sometime, far in the future, the dead shall see heaven. Then, Anne Killigrew can perform her part "As Harbinger of Heav'n, the Way to show" (194).[9]

Like Wasserman, I also believe that Wordsworth's predicament is ours—how to create order and universal meaning.[10] The romantic "imagination" achieves cosmic order within poetry, molding oneness from the diversity of nature, as the poet feels himself merge with infinity. Since external nature no longer contains intrinsic pattern, the poem itself becomes the record of the poet's desire to fix permanently "spots of time"[11] in the moving flux of daily existence. Even in 1928 Virginia Woolf's definition of reality is essentially romantic:[12]

> It would seem to be something very erratic . . . now to be found in a dusty road, now in a scrap of newspaper in the street, now in a daffodil in the sun. . . . whatever it touches, it fixes and makes permanent. That is what remains over when the skin of the day

has been cast into the hedge; that is what is left of past time and of our loves and hates.

Stream of consciousness becomes the most satisfactory way "to fix and make permanent" apprehension of reality in a scrap of newspaper or in a daffodil. No single vision, like *discordia concors*, unifies cosmic disorder; any single point of view is as good as any other. The epic narrator who guides and manipulates the reader's responses throughout *Paradise Lost* is replaced by an author who filters reality through his characters, so that no one vision predominates. Indeed, a multiplicity of views more clearly approximates the truth.

Such radical readjustment to "wit as a kind of *discordia concors*" represented progress to many and the long overdue rectification of ancient errors. Whereas the metaphysical poets believed their conceptual metaphors reflected God's absolute truth, metaphor now reflects a subjective truth: "So much depends," as William Carlos Williams says, "upon / a red wheel / barrow."[13] But the new equation of truth with Baconian "facts" or with empty images intensified by the imagination, represents a flattening of humanity's proper proportions.

The concept of *discordia concors* had long portrayed a finite universe; within a closed system discords might vary, but the tendency toward diversity was always stabilized by the pull toward concord. From its earliest formulation the principle had expressed a harmony born of discord, but in the eighteenth century it is exchanged for a theory of infinite diversity. Infinity, of course, implies unlimited discord, but without the counterbalance of concord. To some the change revealed unchecked chaos and cosmic meaninglessness, to others a panorama of ever-unfolding sublime majesty.[14] The substitution of a theory of infinite diversity for *discordia concors*, the notion of a finitely varied yet harmonious universe, apparently led to two tendencies—the praise of variety for its own sake and alternatively, the praise of homogeneity. In effect, the unity of *discordia concors* is divided in the eighteenth century into its two integral elements: discord and concord. Those who admired the sublimity of infinite diversity espoused variety, and projected their optimism into the very distant future—in progress and in God's grace—while others, perhaps fearing chaos and disorder, approved the customary, the uniform, the general, and the abstract. The ability to enjoy two antithetical possibilities at once is an art virtually lost with the metaphysical poets. Its disappearance may be traced to an occurrence as crucial as the displacement of *discordia concors* as a cosmic theory—the separation of wit into two distinct faculties, judgment and fancy. According to Hobbes's "Answer . . . to . . . D'Avenant's Preface, *Discourse upon Gondibert*" (1650), "Judgement begets the strength and structure, and Fancy begets the ornaments of a Poem."[15] To associate "judgement" with "strength" and "fancy" with "ornaments" suggests the suspicion with which fancy is regarded. Later in the century wit is overtly linked with discerning resemblances while judgment is allied with the more impressive faculty of detecting differences.[16] The diminution of wit into mere fancifulness or wittiness, and its gathering of similitudes, leads to an undue emphasis upon the concord of *discordia concors*.

The gradual inclination among many to approve only the concord of *discordia concors* finds a marked parallel in the distinction of "great thoughts [as] always general."[17] It is not so surprising then to read in Joseph Addison's history of puns that they are deemed "blemishes."[18] Puns are by nature a very compressed form of *discordia concors*, in which two different meanings are yoked together within one word. The "particular" yoked at once with the "general," the discordant with the concordant—so largely admired in the earlier seventeenth century—had become a disfigurement in the eighteenth.

Those who find infinite variety and diversity agreeable become enchanted with the picturesque in nature, seekers after sublime views. After hundreds of years of neglect, the Swiss Alps, for instance, suddenly become objects of awe; nature itself contains moral and theistic lessons for mankind. Mont Blanc inspires Shelley, and the poem comes to symbolize the romantic imagination and its confrontation with the universe. The cultivation of sensibility and taste becomes the proper activity for all those who possess the leisure and affluence to pursue it. Landscape gardens are artfully contrived to appear various and natural; gone is that model of worldly order, the carefully laid rows of flowers and walks, representing cosmic unity to an earlier age; the "industrious Bee" no longer hums there within his "fragrant Zodiack" of herbs and spices, mediating between time and eternity.

Within an adverse environment of increasing rationalism, scientific skepticism, and philosophical materialism, the loss of *discordia concors* as a unifying cosmic principle, informing every aspect of man and nature, destroyed the rationale of metaphysical verse. And the devaluation of wit into mere fancifulness destroyed the means of both yoking "the most heterogeneous ideas" together and of finding oneness in multiplicity. The complex truth expressed by the wit of *discordia concors* was thus gently led to the shade, eclipsed by the light of reason and of progress, and of a new day and the necessity of doing things differently. As Dr. Johnson says in "The Life of Cowley," where we began our discussion: "Wit, like all other things subject by their nature to the choice of man, has its changes and fashions, and at different times takes different forms."[19]

NOTES

CHAPTER ONE

1. For more on the changing concept of wit, see Edward Tayler, introduction to *Literary Criticism of Seventeenth-Century England*, pp. 3-32.
2. See Marjorie Hope Nicolson, *The Breaking of the Circle*. For more on the demise of "correspondence," see, e.g., Victor Harris, *All Coherence Gone*; Hiram Haydn, *The Counter-Renaissance*; C. S. Lewis, *The Discarded Image*; D. C. Allen, *Doubt's Boundless Sea*; and Herschel Baker, *The Wars of Truth*. See also Earl Wasserman's excellent chapter "Metaphors for Poetry" in his *The Subtler Language*.
3. Tayler discusses the division of wit into fancy and judgment in his introduction, pp. 26-27, et passim.
4. See Gracián's *Agudeza y arte de ingenio* (*Conceit and the Art of Wit*), published in 1642; Tesauro's *Il Cannocchiale aristotelico* (*The Aristotelian Telescope*) of 1654. For differing commentaries see S.L. Bethell, "Gracián, Tesauro, and the Nature of Metaphysical Wit," 19-40, and Eugenio Donato, "Tesauro's Poetics," 15-30. The history of the term baroque, including its transition from the fine arts to literature, is well outlined by René Wellek in "The Concept of Baroque in Literary Scholarship" and "Postscript 1962," rpt. in *Concepts of Criticism*, ed. Stephen G. Nichols, Jr., pp. 69-127. For emblems and *imprese* see especially Mario Praz, *Studies in Seventeenth-Century Imagery*. See also Louis L. Martz, *The Poetry of Meditation*; J. A. Mazzeo, "Metaphysical Poetry and the Poetic of Correspondence," 221-34.

Notes

5. "Life of Cowley," 1:14. All quotations are from this edition.
6. I am not the first to use the identification of wit with *discordia concors* as a thematic approach to poetry. I am especially indebted to the stimulation afforded by Wasserman's *The Subtler Language*. See also Edward Lee Piepho's unpublished M.A. essay "The Principle of Concordia Discors and Andrew Marvell's 'The First Anniversary of the Government under O. C.' "; Earl Miner, *The Metaphysical Mode from Donne to Cowley*, usefully, but only partially, clarifies the nature of metaphysical wit as "definition, that is, as those logical or rhetorical processes bringing together or separating (whether in metaphor or idea) matters of similar or opposed classes; and as that dialectic, or those processes, that extend such matters by their relation in logical and rhetorical procedures" (preface, xi-xii). Since *discordia concors* brings together dissimilars or opposites, Miner touches upon the concept in ch. 3, "Wit: Definition and Dialectic," pp. 118-58. George Williamson, *The Proper Wit of Poetry*, quite briefly mentions *discordia concors* in his analysis of Jacobean wit, but I am uncertain if Williamson properly appreciates Dr. Johnson's great insight, because he asserts that the "grounds for all these [Johnson's] remarks are found in [John] Hoskins" (p. 23), and, further, his analyses of Donne's poetry do not depend upon an understanding of *discordia concors*; Frank L. Huntley, "Dr. Johnson and Metaphysical Wit," in *Poetic Theory / Poetic Practice*, ed. Robert Scholes, 103-12. I agree with Huntley that basically two kinds of *discordia concors* prevail, but there are actually more distinctions to be drawn, especially between individual practitioners of metaphysical wit, and neither Huntley nor the critics above make such distinctions.
7. Thomas Hobbes, "The Answer . . . to . . . D Avenant's Preface, *Discourse upon Gondibert*," in Tayler, *Literary Criticism*, p. 287.
8. *The Works of John Milton*, ed. Frank Patterson et al., 11: 103-37.
9. See esp. Johan Huizinga, *The Waning of the Middle Ages*; Walter J. Ong, S. J., "Wit and Mystery," 310-41; C. S. Lewis, *The Discarded Image*.
10. "The Search" 29-30, *Works of George Herbert*, ed. F. E. Hutchinson, p. 163. Further quotations are from this edition.
11. Frag. 112, *Heraclitus*, ed. Philip Wheelwright, p. 90. Subsequent quotations are from this edition. I follow Wheelwright's system of numbering, rather than that of Diels or others.
12. The writings of Pythagoras are not extant. One of the best summaries of his teachings appears in Aristotle's *Metaphysics* (esp. 1.5.2.). See also Kathleen Freeman, *The Pre-Socratic*

Philosophers, p. 82, et passim. For more on harmony see esp. Gretchen Finney, *Musical Backgrounds for English Literature: 1580-1650*, pp. 32-33; and John Hollander, *The Untuning of the Sky . . . ,1500-1700*, p. 27.

13. 1.12.16-19, in *Satires, Epistles, Ars Poetica*, trans. H. R. Fairclough, p. 328.
14. See Ovid, *Metamorphoses* 1.430-34, and Lucius Annaeus Seneca, *Naturales quaestiones* 7.27.3-4.
15. Trans. R[obert] A[shley], fols. 1^r, 1^r, and 6^r, respectively.
16. The belief that discord prevailed throughout life in constant antagonism with concord is a commonplace. See, e.g., the work by the Spanish scholar Juan Luis Vives (1492-1540), *De Concordia & discordia*. . . . Vives deplored the prevalence of discord and prayed that God's grace would bring all to concord. In medieval law, too, one finds the effort to reconcile discord in the "Concordance of Discordant Canons." See esp. Stephan G. Kuttner, *Harmony from Dissonance*.
17. Frag. 23, *The Fragments of Empedocles*, trans. William Ellery Leonard, p. 27.
18. See H. V. S. Ogden, "Principles of Variety and Contrast in Seventeenth-Century Aesthetics, and Milton's Poetry." Ogden is interested in "the principle of contrast" as an "aesthetic theory," especially in relationship to landscape painting (167).
19. "The Dedicatory Epistle," *Poetical Works of Edmund Spenser*, ed. J. C. Smith and E. de Selincourt, p. 417.
20. The writings of Pico della Mirandola make it clear that *discordia concors* was thought an integral element of beauty: "ut concors discordia partium venustas, concors humorum discordia sanitas, concors discordia superorum & inferorum orbium mundi pulchritudo," bk. 3, ch. 9, *Opera* 2:634.
21. 5.178-84, *Complete Poems and Major Prose*, ed. Merritt Y. Hughes, p. 306. All subsequent quotations are from this edition.
22. Samuel Daniel, *A Defence of Rhyme*, in *Elizabethan Critical Essays*, ed. G. Gregory Smith, 2:360.
23. *Poems*, ed. A. R. Waller, 1:253-54. Further quotations from Cowley are from this edition. For more on tuning the discordant soul to a harmony analogous to that in nature, see especially Leo Spitzer's "Classical and Christian Ideas of World Harmony."
24. The pattern of *discordia concors* implicitly suggests a circle, emblem of God's perfection and eternity (Le Roy, fol. 1^r):

    God almighty, maker, and governour of this great worke . . . contayning in himselfe the beginning, the end, and the meanes of all, . . .

Notes

will that it be tempered by alternative chaunges, and maintayned by contraries, his eternal essence remayning alwaies one and unchangeable.

Donne also knew that by taking a common reference point within the circle of God, all differences "meete in one Center" and are resolved:

Here is a new Mathematiques; without change of Elevation, or parallax, I that live in this Climate, and stand under this Meridian, looke up and fixe my self upon God, And they that are under my feete, looke up to that place, which is above them, And as divers, as contrary as our places are, we all fixe at once upon one God, and meete in one Center.

(Quoted from no. 12, *The Sermons of John Donne*, ed. Potter and Simpson, 7:307. This edition is used throughout.)

25. *Discorso intorno a i contrasti, che si fanno sopra la Gerusalemme liberata di Torquato Tasso* (1586), quoted by Bernard Weinberg in *A History of Literary Criticism in the Italian Renaissance* 2:1028-29.
26. P. 22.

Our age loathes simplicity, and . . . requires extravagance in style. . . . Therefore let us speak of sharpness [mental acuity], so that we may accommodate ourselves to the times. . . . Just as material acumen [i.e., wit] is the conjunction of two lines or two sides in one point . . . so acumen [wit] with respect to metaphor is the yoking or disagreeing concord of the subject and the predicate in an oration. . . . Acumen [wit] is *concors discordia* or *discors concordia*.

I first read about Radau in Harvey Goldstein, "*Discordia Concors*, Decorum, and Cowley," a study illuminating the rich tradition of *discordia concors*.

27. Spitzer, "World Harmony," 415. Spitzer's work is an important source for the philosophical background of *discordia concors* and related principles.
28. Frag. 117, op. cit., p. 102.
29. *The Sphere of Marcus Manilius made an English Poem* by Edward Sherburne, p. 13. For the Latin text see *Astronomicon* 1.140-49.
30. See also, e.g., Harris, *All Coherence Gone*; Haydn, *The Counter-Renaissance*; Allen, *Doubt's Boundless Sea*.
31. Lines 391-92, 396, *The Anniversaries*, ed. Frank Manley, p. 79. Further citations of the text are to this edition. To maintain consistent spelling, I have modernized Manley's *i* to *j* and *v* to *u*, or *u* to *v*, as needed.
32. Le Roy, *Variety*, fol. 5^v.

Notes

CHAPTER TWO

1. *The Elegies and the Songs and Sonnets,* ed. Helen Gardner, p. 49. All quotations from the love poetry are from this edition.
2. Donald Guss, *John Donne, Petrarchist*, discusses the Renaissance philosophical traditions that Donne uses throughout his love poetry.
3. S. L. Bethell analyzes the false logic of "The Flea" in "Gracián, Tesauro, and the Nature of Metaphysical Wit," 37-38.
4. See Guss, *John Donne*, esp. pp. 168-69.
5. A. J. Smith, "New Bearings in Donne: 'Air and Angels,' " believes that, despite its brilliance, Dr. Johnson's apprehension of metaphysical poetry as a yoking of heterogeneous ideas has proved detrimental to understanding Donne's verse.
6. N. J. C. Andreasen, for example, in *John Donne*, interprets "The Undertaking" as a genuine appreciation of spiritual love. Contrary elements are dismissed (pp. 204-09).
7. Helen Gardner summarizes the various analyses and adds her own neoplatonic reading in "The Argument about 'The Ecstasy.' "
8. For further discussion of lovers as a microcosm, see Donald Guss, *John Donne, Petrarchist*; also Rosalie Colie, *Paradoxia Epidemica*, ch. 3.
9. Johan Huizinga, *The Waning of the Middle Ages*, p. 202. See esp. his discussion of "symbolic assimilation," pp. 203-04. Herschel Baker, *The Wars of Truth*, pp. 135-86, helpfully comments on the philosophical debate that led to the decline of scholastic realism.
10. *Religio Medici* 1.34, ed. L. C. Martin, p. 33. Hereinafter this work is abbreviated *R.M.* and quotations will be cited parenthetically from this edition.
11. Eugenio Donato, "Tesauro's Poetics" 20, quotes from Emmanuele Tesauro, *Il Cannocchiale aristotelico (The Aristotelian Telescope),* first published in 1654.
12. Eugenio Donato, "Tesauro's Poetics," makes the point that the poet creates a new reality which is essentially true if not identical with external nature (25). Cf. the opposing views of S. L. Bethell, "Gracián, Tesauro, and the Nature of Metaphysical Wit" and J. A. Mazzeo, "Metaphysical Poetry and the Poetic of Correspondence," who believe the poet finds (i.e., "discovers") God's own metaphors in nature. The role of wit, in their view, is merely to discover, rather than create, the correspondence between one thing and another. In my own opinion, however, the growing skepticism of the 1600s hindered, if not prevented, such ready discoveries.

Notes

13. *The Divine Poems*, ed. Helen Gardner, p. 48. I use this edition throughout.
14. "Expostulation" 19, p. 126. All further quotations from the *Devotions* are from this edition. Page references are inserted parenthetically in the text. Out of context italics are hereafter omitted.
15. See esp. Louis Martz, *The Poetry of Meditation*, pp. 34-36, for the three-part structure of a formal meditation and of the soul. Martz discusses the *Anniversaries* at length in ch. 6. Frank Manley, ed., *The Anniversaries*, points out (intro., p. 41) that the triadic structure of the poems corresponds to the traditionally tripartite soul: memory, understanding, and will, which correspond respectively to seeing, judging, and following virtue. See also Rosalie Colie, "Rhetoric of Transcendent Knowledge," in *Paradoxia Epidemica*, pp. 413-29; J. A. Mazzeo, "Notes on John Donne's Alchemical Imagery," in *Renaissance and Seventeenth-Century Studies*, pp. 60-89, for "old and new science"; Louis I. Bredvold's two articles, "The Naturalism of Donne in Relation to Some Renaissance Traditions" and "The Religious Thought of Donne in Relation to Medieval and Later Traditions," for skepticism and decay of nature; Robert Ornstein, "Donne, Montaigne, and Natural Law"; George Williamson, "The Design of Donne's *Anniversaries*," for the poems as companion pieces in the pattern of "question" and "answer" in medieval argument; Rosalie L. Colie, " 'All in Peeces' . . . ," in *Just So Much Honor* . . . , ed. Peter A. Fiore, pp. 189-218; O. B. Hardison, *The Enduring Moment* . . . ; Carol Marks Sicherman, "Donne's Timeless *Anniversaries*"; and Barbara Lewalski, *Donne's Anniversaries and the Poetry of Praise*, a study of the poems' mixed genres which, together, create a new symbolic mode. Professor Lewalski's work appeared after this essay was written, but I wish to note its importance.
16. See Marjorie Hope Nicolson, *The Breaking of the Circle*, pp. 81-122, for her reading of the *Anniversaries* and the theories of the "maiden Queen," Virgin Mary, and Astraea; for *sapientia* see Manley's introduction to his edition of the poems; and for Jonson's "Conversations with William Drummund of Hawthornden," which contain both Jonson's comments and Donne's alleged reply, see the selection in Edward Tayler's *Literary Criticism of Seventeenth-Century England*, p. 84. See also Marius Bewley, "Religious Cynicism in Donne's Poetry," who contends that Elizabeth Drury is a symbol of the Church. In his fine article " 'Essential . . . ' *Anniversaries*" P. G. Stanwood rightly interprets Elizabeth Drury as herself, but he does not see her as the "Idea of a Woman."
17. *The First Anniversary*, in *The Anniversaries*, ed. Frank

Manley, p. 73. All citations from the *First* and *Second Anniversaries* are to this edition, abbreviated *F.A.* and *S.A.* respectively.

18. See esp., Victor Harris, *All Coherence Gone*, pp. 1-7 and 118-28.
19. Trans. from the 2nd ed. by the author, p. 595.
20. Stanwood also notes that the two *Anniversaries* are related like the Old and New Testaments, but he does not elaborate.
21. Cf. Donne's sermon (1618) on Ezek. 33:32, "And lo, thou *art* unto them as a very lovely song . . . ," in *Sermons*, ed. Potter and Simpson, 2:164-78; esp. p. 170, wherein the "instrument" of a disordered world is "tun'd" by God's adding "a new string, *semen mulieris*, the seed of the woman, the *Messias:* And onely by sounding that string . . . become we *musicum carmen*, true musick, true harmony, true peace to you."

CHAPTER THREE

1. *Works of George Herbert*, ed. F. E. Hutchinson, p. 38. Further quotations are from this edition.
2. Margaret Bottrall, *George Herbert*, rightly observes that Herbert's "wit does not depend for its effect upon far-fetched conceits, recondite allusions or reasoned arguments" and therefore is to be distinguished from the wit of Donne, but I disagree with her other conclusion that "there seems to be no good reason for describing [Herbert's verse] as metaphysical" (p. 133). I believe *discordia concors* provides that "reason." See Rosemond Tuve, *A Reading of George Herbert*, who explicates many traditional paradoxes, which leads her also to conclude that Herbert's poetry is not "metaphysical" but I believe it is in Herbert's distinctive use of traditional paradoxes that his metaphysical wit truly emerges.
3. See Rosale Colie, "*Logos* in the Temple," *Paradoxia Epidemica*, pp. 196-97, for her comments on the two "H. Scriptures," which note that "the Book 'matches' whatever experiences a man may have" and in so doing provides a "description and a prescription for every moral particular" (p. 196). She does not amplify these insights but turns elsewhere.
4. The critics have interpreted the "Jordan" poems as a rejection of Petrarchan verse. See esp. Colie, "*Logos*," in *Paradox-*

ia, p. 195; Joseph Summers, *George Herbert*, esp. pp. 108-09; Tuve; and Mary Ellen Rickey, *Utmost Art*, esp. pp. 30-31. I, however, see the poems as an apparent rejection that is ultimately reconciled.

5. For a history of primero see, e.g., the *OED* and Samuel Weller Singer, *Researches into the History of Playing Cards*, esp. pp. 244-48.

CHAPTER FOUR

1. Ross Garner, *Henry Vaughan: Experience and the Tradition*, p. 6. Unfortunately my study was completed before the valuable recent work by James D. Simmonds, *Masques of God*, appeared. I share his view that a revaluation of *Silex Scintillans* is due.

2. *Complete Poetry of Henry Vaughan*, ed. French Fogle, p. 183. All quotations from *Silex Scintillans* are from this edition.

3. *Of Paradise and Light*, pp. 24, 29.

4. See esp. Garner; Elizabeth Holmes, *Henry Vaughan and the Hermetic Philosophy*; R. A. Durr, *On the Mystical Poetry of Henry Vaughan*; and Itrat-Husain, *The Mystical Element in the Metaphysical Poets of the Seventeenth Century*.

5. Pettet, p. 199. P. Jeffrey Ford's "Vision in the Poetry of Henry Vaughan" pursues Pettet's insight, exploring several image clusters in *Silex Scintillans*. I have benefited from Ford's discussions of "Sure, there's a tye of Bodyes!" and "Regeneration," in particular.

6. See Horace H. Underwood, "Time and Space in the Poetry of Henry Vaughan," who rightly observes a "cohesive system" of light-dark imagery, but I question his assertion that "all finite time is night; eternity is day" (p. 231). See also S. Sandbank, "Henry Vaughan's Apology for Darkness," who maintains that the value of darkness is to set off the light by being its opposite. I believe, however, that when a poem is set, as "The Night" is, within an unregenerate context, darkness takes on the customary moral value of light.

7. See St. John [de Yepes] of the Cross, *Complete Works*, trans. and ed. E. Allison Peers, 1:456. Vaughan's allusions to the mystical tradition of the dark night of the soul, found exten-

Notes

sively in the works of St. John of the Cross and others such as Dionysius the Areopagite, have been previously noted by critics. See, e.g., Durr, pp. 119-21.

8. P. 95.
9. Pettet, p. 152.
10. Simmonds (pp. 186-88) also notes the connection between the flower and bed-grave image complex. My primary interest in the association is, however, its ultimate link with "The Night" and Vaughan's creation of "regenerate paradox."
11. Vaughan's relationship to the natural world is controversial. There is little support today for the belief that he was a forerunner of Wordsworth. Elizabeth Holmes argues for a Hermetic reading, since it frees the poet from the label of "Nature-mystic" (*Henry Vaughan and Hermetic Philosophy*, p. 2). Although I disagree with both such theories, I do think Vaughan "presents a Nature *sub specie aeternitatis*, almost without a local habitation" (p. 9)—a notion E. C. Pettet deplores: Vaughan "walked in the fields; they were the Brecon fields; and in them he saw the handiwork of God" (*Of Paradise and Light*, p. 98); Itrat-Husain suggests that "the countryside" is "an Eden on earth" to the poet (*The Mystical Element*, p. 241). Indeed, "God is present as an unseen spirit in nature, but one cannot have the mystic's 'full-eyed' vision of God in nature, and so he longs to 'climb' to God and leave these 'masques and shadows' of His glory in created nature behind" (p. 255). I, however, see no way to redeem visible nature as a good in itself. It is not, in Vaughan's system, to be transcended so that a more perfect, " 'full-eyed' " vision of God may be enjoyed. Rather, nature is false and deceitful, and therefore either to be retreated from or to be transcended and left behind. Vaughan finally rejects nature because it is a false shadow that leads not to God and regeneration, but to vain gadding.
12. *The Mount of Olives: or, Solitary Devotions*, in *The Works of Henry Vaughan*, ed. L. C. Martin, p. 151.

CHAPTER FIVE

1. Since the major portion of Marvell's lyrics were undated and published posthumously, their dating is only approximate. Marvell's editors, the late H. M. Margoliouth and George deF.

Lord, believe that his finest lyrics such as "Upon Appleton House" were written at Nunappleton in Yorkshire during the early 1650s. Close similarity of imagery and themes also suggests that these lyrics derive from this period. In Donne's case less uncertainty exists, since Elizabeth Drury died in 1610 and the *Anniversaries* were published during 1611-12. For a more extensive discussion of dating see Margoliouth, *Poems and Letters of Andrew Marvell*, or the 3rd ed. of Margoliouth by Pierre Legouis; *Andrew Marvell: Complete Poetry*, ed. George deF. Lord, whose text I use throughout; and Frank Manley's introduction to his edition of the *Anniversaries*.

2. *Marvell's Ironic Vision*, p. 124.
3. Ibid., p. 7.
4. For frag. 115 and its interpretation, see *Heraclitus*, ed. Philip Wheelwright, pp. 91, 100. I quote from p. 100.
5. See my discussion, in ch. 2, of Herbert's "The Pulley," pp. 47ff.
6. Toliver, p. 79, has observed the puns on feet and hands.
7. See Donald Friedman, *Marvell's Pastoral Art*, pp. 183-87. Friedman contends that Marvell's "mind is not on the act of sexual consummation, but rather on the symbolic force of the physical union between the lovers" (p. 186). This suggests that symbols are unrelated to life, but I doubt that Marvell's "mind" would divide the "symbol" from the "act." I also must disagree with Friedman when he apparently believes the lovers have successfully conquered time: "life lived so intensely in the moment," he says, "that it seems to subsume eternity itself within a point of time" (p. 187). To me, this is precisely what the lovers do *not* achieve.
8. Frederick L. Gwynn writes in *Explicator* that the sun and "time's winged chariot" suggest the myth of Phaeton; Lawrence Sasek answers Gwynn in *Explicator*; Toliver is uncertain whether the myth is involved (p. 157); see also John Carroll, "The Sun and the Lovers in 'To his Coy Mistress.'"
9. See Edward Tayler, *Nature and Art in Renaissance Literature*, esp. pp. 142-68. Tayler centers the Mower's loss of harmony in the mind and links it to the Fall.
10. "To the immortall memorie, and friendship of that noble paire, Sir Lucius Cary, and Sir. H. Morison," in *Ben Jonson*, ed. Herford, Simpson, and Simpson. 8:243.
11. *Nature and Art*, p. 168. The *hortus conclusus* motif is discussed extensively in Stanley Stewart's *The Enclosed Garden*.
12. *Nature and Art*, p. 166.
13. "Deigne *at my hands this crown of prayer and praise*," *John Donne: The Divine Poems*, ed. Helen Gardner, p. 2.

Notes

14. Miss Colie's mention of the bee as "georgic" (p. 169) reminded me of Virgil, but she does not discuss this.
15. 4.92-102, trans. H. R. Fairclough, 1:203. Further citations are from this edition.
16. "Some Notes on Andrew Marvell's Garden," 121.
17. Toliver, *Ironic Vision*, pp. 150-51.
18. Frank Kermode, "The Argument of Marvell's 'Garden,'" rpt. in *Seventeenth-Century English Poetry: Modern Essays in Criticism*, ed. William R. Keast, p. 313.
19. Patrick Cullen, *Spenser, Marvell, and Renaissance Pastoral*, p. 161, identifies "the milder Sun" of st. 8 with Christ. I prefer, however, to see it as a prefiguration of the Son. Unfortunately, I missed the benefit of reading beforehand Cullen's often perceptive analyses of Marvell and am grateful to Professor Gwynne Evans for calling the book to my attention.
20. "The Starre" 29-32, *Works of George Herbert*, ed. F. E. Hutchinson, p. 74.
21. *Georgics* 4.220-27, 1:211, 213.
22. "The soote season," in *Poems*, ed. Emrys Jones, p. 2.
23. Pierre Legouis, in *Andrew Marvell*, p. 70, is perhaps most explicit about a tripartite structure, and it is he in particular who finds the poem's final four lines so enigmatic. In *Poetry of Meditation*, p. 61, Louis Martz considers "On a Drop of Dew" as a three-part meditation. Toliver presents a more sophisticated reading than Legouis, but he nevertheless tends to interpret the poem in "thirds." For example, he says, "If the second eighteen lines act as the emotional antithesis of the first eighteen, the last four synthesize the two aspects of the descent and return" (p. 75). Like Legouis, Toliver also tends to miss the significance of the "Manna's sacred Dew."
24. 1.11. Martin, p. 11. The significance of tense shifts, especially in Milton's verse, is discussed by Lowry Nelson, Jr., *Baroque Lyric Poetry*.
25. Cf. Milton's use of distorted tenses in "Upon the Circumcision": Christ "Enter'd the world, now bleeds to give us ease" (11), Hughes, p. 81.
26. For more on the theory of accommodation, especially as applied to Milton, see Leland Ryken, *The Apocalyptic Vision in Paradise Lost*.
27. *R.M.* 1.16. The quotation in the following sentence is from the same section.
28. "Life of Cowley," 1:14.
29. Emily Dickinson, "Essential oils are wrung," in *Selected Poems of Emily Dickinson*, ed. James Reeves, pp. 62-63.

Notes

30. No. 4, "Preached at a Christning," *Sermons of John Donne*, ed. Potter and Simpson, 5:97.
31. This is also Virgil's "parvis componere magna solebam," *Ecl.* 1.23.
32. *Index de allegoriis,* in *Patrologia latina,* ed. J.-P. Migne, 219:130.
33. After concluding that manna was linked with Christ and the Eucharist, I read J. E. Saveson's brief but excellent article "Marvel's 'On a Drop of Dew,'" in which Saveson cites Jeremy Taylor to support his belief that manna refers to Christ and the Eucharist (p. 290).
34. *Opera omnia,* in *Patr. lat.,* 112:955.
35. Ibid., 108:869. See also the entry under "dew" in the appendix of *Medieval English Lyrics,* ed. R. T. Davies, p. 372.
36. Trans. C. A., pp. 118-19.
37. "Three Academic Pieces," *The Necessary Angel,* p. 72.
38. John Donne, *Sermons,* no. 8, 5:169.
39. Rosalie Colie, *Paradoxia Epidemica,* p. 282, observes that the dew is a mirror that invites "speculation."

CHAPTER SIX

1. *Areopagitica,* Hughes, p. 728.
2. T. S. Eliot, "Milton," 75.
3. F. R. Leavis, *The Common Pursuit,* p. 22.
4. "The Miltonic Simile." The "homologation" quotation is from 1034; the diagram, 1043.
5. Cf. Whaler's Satan-leviathan diagram, 1050.
6. James Patterson, *A Complete Commentary . . . on Milton's Paradise Lost,* p. 42.
7. See D. M. Hill, "Satan on the Burning Lake."
8. Milton, *Areopagitica,* p. 728.
9. See Kingsley Widmer, "The Iconography of Renunciation: The Miltonic Simile," esp. 259.
10. *Milton's Epic Voice,* esp. pp. 67-88.
11. Douglas Bush, "Ironic and Ambiguous Allusion in 'Paradise Lost,'" 635.
12. *Milton's Grand Style,* p. 129.

Notes

13. *Paradise Lost as "Myth,"* chs. 2-3. See also Jackson I. Cope, *The Metaphoric Structure of Paradise Lost*, esp. the ch. "Scenic Structure."
14. A. J. A. Waldock, *Paradise Lost and Its Critics*, p. 87. See also John Peter, *A Critique of Paradise Lost*.
15. *Areopagitica*, pp. 741-42.
16. Ibid., p. 742.
17. Frag. 108, *Heraclitus*, Wheelwright, p. 90.
18. See also John Steadman, "Image and Idol in 'Paradise Lost,'" who notes "eidolon" and Satan's pretensions to godhead (p. 652). Steadman is not discussing similes, but various types of illusion, such as Eve's vulnerability to her own reflection in the lake.
19. See esp. Cope, *Metaphoric Structure of P.L.*, pp. 130-48, for the Fall at noon and Satan as the "midday devil"; also Albert R. Cirillo, "Noon-Midnight and the Temporal Structure of *Paradise Lost*."
20. See Cleanth Brooks, "Milton and the New Criticism," esp. for the discussion of the "disastrous twilight" which the eclipse portends.
21. After writing this chapter I noted that Cope also saw the parallel between Satan and Samson (p. 99).
22. For more on this observation see Ricks, *Milton's Grand Style*, esp. the section "Words, Actions, All Infect," pp. 109-17.
23. Quotations in this paragraph are from *The Interpretation of Dreams*, trans. and ed. James Strachey, pp. 471, 318, 319, respectively.
24. *Areopagitica*, p. 728.
25. Ibid., p. 744. For more on *Areopagitica* and the importance of choosing well, see MacCaffrey, *P.L., as "Myth,"* esp. pp. 33, 210.
26. See his "Structural Pattern in *Paradise Lost*," rpt. in *Milton: Modern Essays in Criticism*, ed. Arthur E. Barker, esp. p. 146.

CHAPTER SEVEN

1. "The Language of Paradox: 'The Canonization,'" in *The Well-Wrought Urn*, rpt. *John Donne: A Collection of Critical Essays*, ed. Helen Gardner, p. 107.
2. Earl R. Wasserman, *The Subtler Language*. "Cooper's

Notes

Hill" and "Windsor Forest" are discussed, pp. 35-168. I should make clear that since Wasserman does not distinguish between different patterns of *discordia concors*, I myself think that his valuable readings of Pope, especially, fit what I have called the Horatian or nontranscendent version of unity in multiplicity. See also Wasserman's "Metaphors for Poetry," which deals with the decline of *discordia concors*. I particularly benefited from his belief that a theory of infinite diversity and variety led to a gradual enervation of the ancient concept. Quotations from Wasserman are cited parenthetically within the text.

3. I paraphrase and share Wasserman's belief that the decline of *discordia concors* is related to the attenuation of certain commonly shared symbols and cosmic theories. See *Subtler Language*, p. 172, et passim. I also agree with his argument that romantic poetry tries to create universal order where it is feared none is.

4. *Complete Poems and Major Prose*, Hughes, p. 728.

5. Ed. Richard Foster Jones, p. 248. Further quotations are from this edition.

6. *Magna Instauratio* (Aphorism 104), p. 316.

7. Ibid., p. 317.

8. *Ben Jonson*, Herford and Simpson, 8:636.

9. *Poems of John Dryden*, ed. James Kinsley, 1:465. The term "Mrs" did not then always signify a married woman.

10. See *The Subtler Language*, esp. p. 186, for further discussion.

11. William Wordsworth, *The Prelude* (text of 1850, 12:208), ed. Carlos Baker, p. 409.

12. *A Room of One's Own*, pp. 113-14.

13. "The Red Wheelbarrow," *The Imagist Poem*, ed. William Pratt, p. 79.

14. See Wasserman, esp. pp. 175-78, for more on infinitude and variety.

15. Thomas Hobbes, in *Literary Criticism of Seventeenth-Century England*, ed. Edward Tayler, p. 283.

16. For more on the disparagement of wit in the later seventeenth century, see Edward Tayler, introduction to *Literary Criticism*, esp. p. 30.

17. Samuel Johnson, "Life of Cowley," *Lives of the English Poets* 1:14.

18. *The Spectator*, ed. Gregory Smith, 1:188.

19. *Lives of the English Poets* 1:12.

WORKS CITED

Addison, Joseph and Richard Steele. *The Spectator.* Ed. Gregory Smith. Vol. 1. 1907. Reprint. London: Everyman's Library–J. M. Dent, 1964.

Allen, D. C. *Doubt's Boundless Sea: Skepticism and Faith in the Renaissance.* Baltimore: The Johns Hopkins Press, 1964.

Andreasen, N. J. C. *John Donne: Conservative Revolutionary.* Princeton: Princeton University Press, 1967.

Aristotle. *Metaphysics.* Trans. Hugh Tredennick. Vol. 1. Cambridge: Loeb Classical Library–Harvard University Press, 1933.

Bacon, Francis, first Baron Verulam and Viscount St. Albans. *Francis Bacon: Essays, Advancement of Learning, New Atlantis, and Other Pieces.* Ed. Richard Foster Jones, New York: Odyssey Press, 1937.

Baker, Herschel. *The Wars of Truth: Studies in the Decay of Christian Humanism in the Earlier Seventeenth Century.* Cambridge: Harvard University Press, 1952.

Barker, Arthur E. "Structural Pattern in *Paradise Lost.*" *Philological Quarterly* 28 (1949): 17-30. Reprinted in *Milton: Modern Essays in Criticism.* Ed. Arthur E. Barker, pp. 142-55. 1965. Reprint. New York: Galaxy–Oxford University Press, 1966.

Bethell, S. L. "Gracián, Tesauro, and the Nature of Metaphysical Wit." *Northern Miscellany of Literary Criticism* no. 1 (autumn 1953): 19-40.

Bewley, Marius. "Religious Cynicism in Donne's Poetry." *Kenyon Review* 14 (1952): 619-46.

Bottrall, Margaret. *George Herbert.* London: John Murray, 1954.

Works Cited

Bredvold, Louis I. "The Naturalism of Donne in Relation to Some Renaissance Traditions." *JEGP* 22 (1923): 471-502.

———. "The Religious Thought of Donne in Relation to Medieval and Later Traditions." *University of Michigan Publications in Language and Literature* 1 (1925): 193-232.

Brooks, Cleanth. "The Language of Paradox: 'The Canonization.' " *The Well-Wrought Urn*. New York: Harcourt, Brace & World, 1947. Reprinted in *John Donne: A Collection of Critical Essays*. Ed. Helen Gardner, pp. 100-108. Englewood Cliffs, N. J.: Prentice-Hall, 1962.

———. "Milton and the New Criticism." *Sewanee Review* 59 (1951): 1-22.

Browne, Sir Thomas. *Religio Medici and Other Works*. Ed. L. C. Martin. Oxford: Clarendon Press, 1964.

Bush, Douglas. "Ironic and Ambiguous Allusion in 'Paradise Lost.' " *JEGP* 60 (1961): 631-40.

Carroll, John. "The Sun and the Lovers in 'To his Coy Mistress.' " *MLN* 74 (1959): 4-7.

Cirillo, Albert. "Noon-Midnight and the Temporal Structure of *Paradise Lost*." *ELH* 29 (1962): 372-95.

Colie, Rosalie L. " 'All in Peeces': Problems of Interpretation in Donne's Anniversary Poems." In *Just So Much Honor: Essays Commemorating the Four-Hundredth Anniversary of the Birth of John Donne*. Ed. Peter A. Fiore. University Park, Pa.: Pennsylvania State University Press, 1972.

———. *"My Ecchoing Song": Andrew Marvell's Poetry of Criticism*. Princeton: Princeton University Press, 1970.

———. *Paradoxia Epidemica: The Renaissance Tradition of Paradox*. Princeton: Princeton University Press, 1966.

Cope, Jackson I. *The Metaphoric Structure of Paradise Lost*. 1962. Reprint. Baltimore: The Johns Hopkins Press, 1964.

Cowley, Abraham. *Poems: Miscellanies, The Mistress, Pindarique Odes, Davideis, Verses Written upon Several Occasions*. Ed. A. R. Waller. Vol. 1. Cambridge: Cambridge University Press, 1905.

Cullen, Patrick. *Spenser, Marvell, and Renaissance Pastoral*. Cambridge: Harvard University Press, 1970.

Daneau, Lambert. *The Wonderfull Woorkmanship of the World*. Englished by T[homas] T[wyne]. London, 1578.

Daniel, Samuel. *A Defence of Rhyme*. In *Elizabethan Critical Essays*. Ed. G. Gregory Smith. Vol. 2. Oxford: Clarendon Press, 1904.

Davies, R. T., ed. *Medieval English Lyrics: A Critical Anthology*. Evanston, Ill.: Northwestern University Press, 1964.

Works Cited

Dickinson, Emily. *Selected Poems of Emily Dickinson*. Ed. James Reeves. 1959. Reprint. London: Heinemann, 1960.

Donato, Eugenio. "Tesauro's Poetics: Through the Looking Glass." *MLN* 78 (1963): 15-30.

Donne, John. *The Anniversaries*. Ed. Frank Manley. Baltimore: The Johns Hopkins Press, 1963.

———. *Devotions upon Emergent Occasions*. 1959. Reprint. Ann Arbor: University of Michigan Press, 1965.

———. *The Divine Poems*. Ed. Helen Gardner. 1952. Reprint. Oxford: Clarendon Press, 1969.

———. *The Elegies and the Songs and Sonnets*. Ed. Helen Gardner. 1965. Reprint. Oxford: Clarendon Press, 1970.

———. *The Sermons*. Ed. George R. Potter and Evelyn M. Simpson. 10 vols. Berkeley: University of California Press, 1953-62.

Dryden, John. *The Poems of John Dryden*. Ed. James Kinsley. Vol. 1. Oxford: Clarendon Press, 1958.

Durr, Robert Allen. *On the Mystical Poetry of Henry Vaughan*. Cambridge: Harvard University Press, 1962.

E. K. "The Epistle Dedicatory to the Shepheardes Calender." In *The Poetical Works of Edmund Spenser*. Ed. J. C. Smith and Ernest de Selincourt. 1912. Reprint. London: Oxford University Press, 1961.

Eliot, T. S. "Milton." *Proceedings of the British Academy* 33 (1947): 61-79.

Empedocles. *The Fragments of Empedocles*. Trans. William Ellery Leonard. Chicago: Open Court Publishing Company, 1908.

Ferry, Ann Davidson. *Milton's Epic Voice: The Narrator in Paradise Lost*. Cambridge: Harvard University Press, 1963.

Finney, Gretchen Ludke. *Musical Backgrounds for English Literaure: 1580-1650*. New Brunswick, N. J.: Rutgers University Press, 1961.

Fish, Stanley E. *Surprised by Sin: The Reader in Paradise Lost*. 1967. Reprint. Berkeley: University of California Press, 1971.

Ford, P. Jeffrey. "Vision in the Poetry of Henry Vaughan." Unpublished M.A. essay, Columbia University, 1965.

Freeman, Kathleen. *The Pre-Socratic Philosophers: A Companion to Diels, Fragmente der Vorsokratiker*. 2nd ed. 1959. Reprint. Cambridge: Harvard University Press, 1966.

Freud, Sigmund. *The Interpretation of Dreams*. Ed. and trans. James Strachey. London: George Allen and Unwin, 1961.

Friedman, Donald M. *Marvell's Pastoral Art*. Berkeley: University of California Press, 1970.

Works Cited

Gardner, Helen. "The Argument about 'The Ecstasy.'" *Elizabethan and Jacobean Studies: Presented to Frank Percy Wilson in Honour of his Seventieth Birthday*, pp. 279-306. Oxford: Clarendon Press, 1959.

Garner, Ross. *Henry Vaughan: Experience and the Tradition.* Chicago: University of Chicago Press, 1959.

Goldstein, Harvey. "*Discordia Concors*, Decorum, and Cowley," *English Studies* 49 (1968): 481-89.

Gracián, Baltasar. *Agudeza y arte de ingenio.* In *Obras completas.* Ed. E. Correa Calderon. Madrid: M. Aguilar, 1944.

Guss, Donald L. *John Donne, Petrarchist: Italianate Conceits and Love Theory in the Songs and Sonets.* Detroit: Wayne State University Press, 1966.

Gwynn, Frederick L. "Marvell's 'To his Coy Mistress.'" *Explicator* 11 (May 1953), no. 7.

Hardison, O. B. *The Enduring Moment: A Study of the Idea of Praise in Renaissance Literary Theory and Practice.* Chapel Hill: University of North Carolina Press, 1962.

Harris, Victor. *All Coherence Gone.* Chicago: University of Chicago Press, 1949.

Hawkins, Henry. *Parthenia sacra, or, the Mysterious and Delicious Garden of the Sacred Parthenes.* Rouen, 1633.

Haydn, Hiram. *The Counter-Renaissance.* 1950. Reprint. New York: Harbinger–Harcourt, Brace & World, n.d.

Heraclitus. *Heraclitus.* Ed. Philip Wheelwright, 1959. Reprint. New York: Atheneum Publishers, 1968.

Herbert, George. *The Works of George Herbert.* Ed. F. E. Hutchinson. 1941. Reprint. Oxford: Clarendon Press, 1967.

Hill, D. M. "Satan on the Burning Lake." *Notes & Queries* n. s. 3 (1956): 157-59.

Hobbes, Thomas. "The Answer . . . to . . . D'Avenant's Preface, *Discourse upon Gondibert.*" In *Literary Criticism of Seventeenth-Century England.* Ed. Edward W. Tayler. Vol. 4 of *The Borzoi Anthology of 17th-Century English Literature*, ed. Joseph A. Mazzeo. New York: Alfred A. Knopf, 1967.

Hollander, John. *The Untuning of the Sky: Ideas of Music in English Poetry, 1500-1700.* Princeton: Princeton University Press, 1961.

Holmes, Elizabeth. *Henry Vaughan and the Hermetic Philosophy.* Oxford: Basil Blackwell, 1932.

Horace. *Satires, Epistles, and Ars Poetica.* Trans. H. R. Fairclough. 1926. Reprint. Cambridge: Loeb Classical Library–Harvard University Press, 1966.

Hoskins, John. *Directions for Speech and Style.* Ed. Hoyt H.

Works Cited

Hudson. Princeton Studies in English, no. 12. Princeton University Press, 1935.

Hugo, Hermann. *Pia desideria: or Divine Addresses, in three books*. Englished by Edmund Arwaker. London, 1690.

Huizinga, Johan. *The Waning of the Middle Ages*. [lst English ed. 1949.] New York: Anchor-Doubleday, 1954.

Huntley, Frank L. "Dr. Johnson and Metaphysical Wit; or, *Discordia Concors* Yoked and Balanced." In *Poetic Theory / Poetic Practice*. Ed. Robert Scholes. Papers of the Midwest Modern Language Association, no. 1 (1969): 103-12.

Itrat-Husain. *The Mystical Element in the Metaphysical Poets of the Seventeenth Century*. 1948. Reprint New York: Biblo and Tannen, 1966.

John [de Yepes] of the Cross, Saint. *The Complete Works of St. John of the Cross*. Ed. and trans. E. Allison Peers. Vol. 1. Rev. ed. London: Burns, Oates & Washbourne, 1953.

Johnson, Samuel. "Life of Cowley." In *Lives of the English Poets*. Vol. 1. 1906. Reprint. London: World's Classics–Oxford University Press, 1964.

Jonson, Ben. *Ben Jonson*. Ed. C. H. Herford, Percy and Evelyn Simpson. Vol. 8. 1947. Reprint. Oxford: Clarendon Press, 1965.

―――. "Ben Jonson's Conversations with William Drummond of Hawthornden." In *Literary Criticism of Seventeenth-Century England*. Ed. Edward W. Tayler. Vol. 4 of *The Borzoi Anthology of 17th-Century English Literature*, ed. Joseph A. Mazzeo. New York: Alfred A. Knopf, 1967.

Kermode, Frank. "The Argument of Marvell's 'Garden.' " *Essays in Criticism* 2 (1952): 225-41. Reprinted in *Seventeenth-Century English Poetry: Modern Essays in Criticism*. Ed. William R. Keast, pp. 290-304. 1962. Reprint. New York: Galaxy–Oxford University Press, 1968.

King, A. H. "Some Notes on Andrew Marvell's Garden." *English Studies* 20 (1938): 118-21.

Kuttner, Stephan G. *Harmony from Dissonance: An Interpretation of Medieval Canon Law*. Latrobe, Pa.: Archabbey Press, 1960.

La Primaudaye, Pierre de. *The Second Part of the French Académie*. Trans. from the 2nd. ed. by the author. London, 1605.

Leavis, F. R. *The Common Pursuit*. 1952. Reprint. Harmondsworth, England: Peregrine–Penguin, 1963.

Legouis, Pierre. *Andrew Marvell: Poet, Puritan, Patriot*. Oxford: Clarendon Press, 1965.

Le Roy, Louis. *Of the Interchangeable Course, or Variety of Things in the Whole World*. Trans. R[obert] A[shley]. London, 1594.

Works Cited

Lewalski, Barbara Kiefer. *Donne's Anniversaries and the Poetry of Praise: The Creation of a Symbolic Mode.* Princeton: Princeton University Press, 1973.

Lewis, C. S. *The Discarded Image: An Introduction to Medieval and Renaissance Literature.* Cambridge: Cambridge University Press, 1964.

MacCaffrey, Isabel Gamble. *Paradise Lost as "Myth."* Cambridge: Harvard University Press, 1959.

Manilius. *Astronomicon. Liber primus.* Ed. A. E. Housman. Cambridge: Cambridge University Press, 1937.

―――. *The Sphere of Marcus Manilius Made an English Poem with Annotations and an Astronomical Appendix* by Edward Sherburne. London, 1675.

Martz, Louis. *The Poetry of Meditation: A Study in English Religious Literature of the Seventeenth Century.* 2nd ed. 1962. Reprint. New Haven: Yale University Press, 1965.

Marvell, Andrew. *The Poems and Letters of Andrew Marvell.* Ed. H. M. Margoliouth. 2 vols. 2nd ed. Oxford: Clarendon Press, 1952.

―――. *The Poems and Letters of Andrew Marvell.* Ed. H. M. Margoliouth and Pierre Legouis. 2 vols. 3rd ed. Oxford: Clarendon Press, 1971.

―――. *Andrew Marvell: Complete Poetry.* Ed. George deF. Lord. New York: Modern Library–Random House, 1968.

Maurus, Rabanus. *Opera omnia.* In *Patrologiae . . . latina.* 2nd ser. Ed. J.-P. Migne. Vols. 108, 112. Paris, 1852.

Mazzeo, Joseph A. "Metaphysical Poetry and the Poetic of Correspondence." *Journal of the History of Ideas* 14 (1953): 221-34.

―――. "Notes on John Donne's Alchemical Imagery." *Renaissance and Seventeenth-Century Studies,* pp. 60-89. New York: Columbia University Press, 1964.

Migne, J.-P. *Index de allegoriis.* In *Patrologiae . . . latina.* 2nd ser. Vol. 219. Paris, 1852.

Milton, John. *The Art of Logic. The Works of John Milton.* Ed. Frank Patterson et al. Vol. 11. New York: Columbia University Press, 1935.

―――. *John Milton: The Complete Poems and Major Prose.* Ed. Merritt Y. Hughes. New York: Odyssey Press, 1957.

Miner, Earl. *The Metaphysical Mode from Donne to Cowley.* Princeton: Princeton University Press, 1969.

Nelson, Lowry, Jr. *Baroque Lyric Poetry.* New Haven: Yale University Press, 1961.

Newton, John. *An Introduction to the Art of Rhetorick.* London, 1671.

Works Cited

Nicolson, Marjorie Hope. *The Breaking of the Circle: Studies in the Effect of the "New Science" upon Seventeenth-Century Poetry.* 1950. Rev. ed. New York: Columbia University Press, 1960.

Ogden, H. V. S. "Principles of Variety and Contrast in Seventeenth-Century Aesthetics, and Milton's Poetry." *Journal of the History of Ideas* 10 (1949): 159-82.

Ong, Walter J., S.J. "Wit and Mystery: A Revaluation in Medieval Latin Hymnody." *Speculum* 22 (1947): 310-41.

Ornstein, Robert M. "Donne, Montaigne, and Natural Law." *JEGP* 55 (1956): 213-29.

Ovid. *Metamorphoses.* Trans. F. J. Miller. 2 vols. Cambridge: Loeb Classical Library-Harvard University Press, 1936.

Patterson, James. *A Complete Commentary, with Etymological, Explanatory, Critical, and Classical Notes on Milton's Paradise Lost.* London, 1744.

Peter, John. *A Critique of Paradise Lost.* New York: Columbia University Press, 1960.

Pettet, E. C. *Of Paradise and Light: A Study of Vaughan's Silex Scintillans.* Cambridge: Cambridge University Press, 1960.

Pico della Mirandola, Giovanni. *Opera quae extant omnia.* Vol. 2 Basel, 1601.

Piepho, Edward␣Lee. "The Principle of Concordia Discors and Andrew Marvell's 'The First Anniversary of the Government under O. C. ' " Unpublished M.A. essay, Columbia University, 1966.

Plato, *Timaeus. The Dialogues of Plato.* Trans. Benjamin Jowett. Vol. 2. Reprinted from the 3rd ed. New York: Random House, 1937.

Praz, Mario. *Studies in Seventeenth-Century Imagery: Second Edition Considerably Increased.* 2nd ed. Rome: Edizioni di Storia e Letteratura, 1964.

Radau, Michael. *Orator extemporaneus.* London, 1673.

Richome, Lewis. *Holy Pictures of the mysticall Figures of the most holy Sacrifice and Sacrament of the Eucharist.* Trans. C. A. n.p., 1619.

Rickey, Mary Ellen. *Utmost Art: Complexity in the Verse of George Herbert.* Lexington, Ky.: University of Kentucky Press, 1966.

Ricks, Christopher. *Milton's Grand Style.* 1963. Reprint. Oxford: Clarendon Press, 1965.

Ryken, Leland. *The Apocalyptic Vision in Paradise Lost.* Ithaca, N. Y.: Cornell University Press, 1970.

Sandbank, S. "Henry Vaughan's Apology for Darkness." *Studies in English Literature: 1500-1900* 7 (1967): 141-52.

Works Cited

Sasek, Lawrence. "Marvell's 'To his Coy Mistress,' 45-46." *Explicator* 14 (April 1956): item 47.

Saveson, J. E. "Marvell's 'On a Drop of Dew.' " *Notes & Queries* n. s. 5 (July 1958): 289-90.

Seneca, Lucius Annaeus. *Naturales quaestiones*. In *Opera quae supersunt*. Ed. Alfred Gercke. Vol. 2. Leipzig: G. B. Teubner, 1907.

Sicherman, Carol Marks. "Donne's Timeless *Anniversaries*." *University of Toronto Quarterly* 39 (1970): 126-43.

Simmonds, James D. *Masques of God: Form and Theme in the Poetry of Henry Vaughan*. Pittsburgh: University of Pittsburgh Press, 1972.

Singer, Samuel Weller. *Researches into the History of Playing Cards; with Illustrations of the Origin of Printing and Engraving on Wood*. London, 1816.

Smith, A. J. "New Bearings in Donne: 'Air and Angels.' " *English* 13 (1960). Reprinted in *John Donne: A Collection of Critical Essays*, ed. Helen Gardner, pp. 171-79. Englewood Cliffs, N. J.: Prentice-Hall, 1962.

Spenser, Edmund. *The Poetical Works of Edmund Spenser*. Ed. J. C. Smith and Ernest de Selincourt. 1912. Reprint. London: Oxford University Press, 1961.

Spitzer, Leo. "Classical and Christian Ideas of World Harmony." *Traditio* 2 (1944): 409-65; 3 (1945): 307-64. Reprint. Baltimore: The Johns Hopkins Press, 1963.

Stanwood, P. G. " 'Essentiall Joye' in Donne's *Anniversaries*." *Texas Studies in Literature and Language* 13 (1971): 227-38.

Steadman, John. "Image and Idol in 'Paradise Lost.' " *JEGP* 59 (1960): 640-54. Reprinted in *Milton's Epic Characters: Image and Idol*. Chapel Hill: University of North Carolina Press, 1968.

Stevens, Wallace. "Three Academic Pieces." *The Necessary Angel: Essays on Reality and the Imagination*. 1942. Reprint. New York: Vintage-Random House, 1965.

Stewart, Stanley. *The Enclosed Garden: The Tradition and the Image in Seventeenth-Century Poetry*. Madison, Wis.: University of Wisconsin Press, 1966.

Summers, Joseph. *George Herbert: His Religion and His Art*. London: Chatto and Windus, 1954.

Surrey, Henry Howard, Earl of. *Poems*. Ed. Emrys Jones. Clarendon Medieval and Tudor Series. Oxford: Clarendon Press, 1964.

Tayler, Edward William. *Nature and Art in Renaissance Literature*. 1964. Reprint. New York: Columbia University Press, 1966.

―――. ed. *Literary Criticism of Seventeenth-Century England*. Vol. 4 of *The Borzoi Anthology of 17th-Century English Literature*,

Works Cited

ed. Joseph Mazzeo. New York: Alfred A. Knopf, 1967.

Tesauro, Emmanuele. *Il Cannocchiale aristotelico.* Turin, 1654.

Toliver, Harold. *Marvell's Ironic Vision.* New Haven: Yale University Press, 1965.

Tuve, Rosemond. *A Reading of George Herbert.* Chicago: University of Chicago Press, 1952.

Underwood, Horace H. "Time and Space in the Poetry of Vaughan." *Studies in Philology* 69 (1972): 231-41.

Vaughan, Henry. *The Complete Poetry of Henry Vaughan.* Ed. French Fogle. 1964. Reprint. New York: W. W. Norton, 1969.

―――. *The Mount of Olives: or, Solitary Devotions.* In *The Complete Works of Henry Vaughan.* Ed. L. C. Martin. 2nd ed. 1957. Reprint. Oxford: Clarendon Press, 1968.

Virgil. *Eclogues, Georgics, and the Aeneid.* Trans. H. R. Fairclough. 2 vols. 2nd ed. 1935. Reprint. Cambridge: Loeb Classical Library–Harvard University Press, 1946.

Vives, Juan Luis. *De concordia & discordia in humano genere ad Carolum v. Caesaerum libri quattuor.* In *Opera omnia.* 1529. Reprint. London: Gregg Press, 1964.

Waldock, A. J. A. *Paradise Lost and Its Critics.* 1947. Reprint. Cambridge: Cambridge University Press, 1962.

Wasserman, Earl R. *The Subtler Language: Critical Readings of Neoclassic and Romantic Poems.* 1959. Reprint. Baltimore: The Johns Hopkins Press, 1968.

Weinberg, Bernard. *A History of Literary Criticism in the Italian Renaissance.* 2 vols. Chicago: University of Chicago Press, 1961.

Wellek, René. "The Concept of Baroque in Literary Scholarship." *Journal of Aesthetics and Art Criticism* 5 (1946): 77-109, and "Postscript 1962." Reprinted in *Concepts of Criticism.* Ed. Stephen G. Nichols, Jr., pp. 69-127. New Haven: Yale University Press, 1963.

Whaler, James. "The Miltonic Simile." *PMLA* 46 (1931): 1034-74.

Widmer, Kingsley. "The Iconography of Renunciation: The Miltonic Simile." *ELH* 25 (1958): 258-69.

Williams, William Carlos. "The Red Wheelbarrow." In *The Imagist Poets: Modern Poetry in Miniature.* Ed. William Pratt. New York: E. P. Dutton, 1963.

Williamson, George. "The Design of Donne's *Anniversaries.*" *Modern Philology* 60 (1963): 183-91.

―――. *The Proper Wit of Poetry.* London: Faber & Faber, 1961.

Woolf, Virginia. *A Room of One's Own.* 1929. Reprint. New York: Harbinger–Harcourt, Brace & World, 1963.

INDEX

Accomodation, theory of, 91; *see also* Ryken, Leland
Addison, Joseph, 134
Aeneid (Virgil), 103
"Aire and Angels" (Donne), 16–17
Allen, Don Cameron, 137, 140
"Altar, The" (Herbert), 53
Ambiguity of mind: as nature of truth, 131; as hindrance to understanding, 131
Ambiguity of words, functional, 33–34, 84, 89, 90, 108, 121
Andreasen, N. J. C., 141
Annihilation, as cure to mortality, in Marvell, 72–73, 76, 80–81, 87–88; *see also* "On a Drop of Dew"
Anniversaries, The (Donne), 12, 25–36, 55, 71, 126, 142; Jonson's comments on, 25; scholarship on, 142
"Answer, The" (Herbert), 48–49
Anniversary, The Second (Donne), 39, 72, 87, 91, 132
Appearance vs. reality: in Vaughan, 61–70, 127; *see also* Illusion
Areopagite, Dionysius the, 145
Areopagitica (Milton), 103–04, 111, 119–20, 131
Art, as natural, 80
Art of Logic, The (Milton), 5
Art of Rhetoric, The (Newton), 11
"Avarice" (Herbert), 40

Bacon, Sir Francis, 130, 131–32
"Bag, The" (Herbert), 51
Baker, Herschel, 137, 141
Barker, Arthur E., 123, 149
Baroque, 4, 137
Beauty: E. K. on, 9; *discordia concors* the integral element of, 139
Beaux' Stratagem, The (Farquhar), 4
"Bermudas" (Marvell), 85–87
Bethell, S. L., 137, 141
Bewley, Marius, 142
Book of Nature, 20, 21, 26, 34–35, Vaughan's controversial reading of, 66–67, 145
Bottrall, Margaret, 143
Bredvold, Louis, 142
Brooks, Cleanth, 114–15, 126, 149
Browne, Sir Thomas, 20–21, 24, 40, 89–90, 91–92, 112
Bush, Douglas, 101–02

"Canonization, The" (Donne), 17, 19, 126
Carmen musicum, 28, 143
Carroll, John, 146

"Cary-Morison Ode" (Jonson), 79
Choosing well, importance of, 112, 119–20, 149
"Church-Porch, The" (Herbert), 47
Christ: as harmonizer, 8, 28, 34; as *carmen musicum*, 28, 143; as *Oriens*, 93; as dew, manna, symbol of Eucharist, and "Almighty Sun," *see* "On a Drop of Dew"; as sun, *see* Miltonic similes
Circle, *see* Structure; *see also* Time and Eternity
Circle of Perfection, 3; *see also* Correspondence
Cirillo, Albert, 149
Colie, Rosalie, 83, 141, 143, 147, 148
"Come, come, what doe I here?" (Vaughan), 64
Complexities, false, *see* Games
Conceit, metaphysical, 4
"Concordance of Discordant Canons," 139
"Confession" (Herbert), 51
Congreve, William, 3
Consciousness, stream of, 133; *see also* Reality
"Content" (Vaughan), 67
Contrast, as aesthetic principle, 8–9
Contrariety: poetic responses to, 11–13, 125–30; *see also* Transcendence
"Cooper's Hill" (Denham), 5, 129
Cope, Jackson I., 149
Corona, La (Donne), 82
"Coronet, The" (Marvell), 45, 88
Correspondence, as world-view, 3–4, 13, 137; demise of, 130–31, 137; *see also* Book of Nature
"Correspondence, Poetic of," 4, 137; *see also* Mazzeo, J. A.
"Corruption" (Vaughan), 62
Courtly love, 15, 41; *see also* Petrarchan love
Cowley, Abraham, 10; *see also* "The Life of Cowley"
"Crosse, The" (Herbert), 49
Cullen, Patrick, 147

Damon the Mower (character in Marvell's verse), 77–78, 80
"Damon the Mower" (Marvell), 77–78
"Dampe, The" (Donne), 14–15
Daneau, Lambert, 9–10
Daniel, Samuel, 139
Dark night of the soul, 58, 69, 144–45
Davideis (Cowley), 10
Davies, R. T., 148
"Definition of Love, The" (Marvell), 75–76, 78

Index

Denham, Sir John, 5, 129–30
Devotions upon Emergent Occasions (Donne), 23–24, 38
Dew: paradoxical quality of, 92; symbolic and biblical references to, 95–96, 148; *see also* "On a Drop of Dew"
"Dew, On a Drop of" (Marvell), 84, 87–97, 98, 128
"Dialogue, between The Resolved Soul and Created Pleasure, A" (Marvell), 73–74, 85
"Dialogue between the Soul and Body, A" (Marvell), 74, 78
Discordant soul tuned, 10, 139; *see also* Spitzer, Leo
Discordia concors: as oxymoron associated with paradox, pun, contraries, 4; major branches of, 5–6; spectrum of idea analogous to dissentaneous arguments of Renaissance logic, 5–6; philosophical background of, 4–8, 140; ancient cosmological principle of, 6–7, 11–12; cosmological analogues to violent yoking of opposites, 11–13; as world composed of harmonious number, weight, and measure, 7–10, 123; art a reflection of, 8–9; beauty as, 9, 139; equation of wit with, 4–5, 11; application of philosophical concept to literary style, 4–5, 8–13; informing element of metaphysical wit as, 4–5, 12–13, 126; as reflection of ambivalent tensions within life, 12–13, 14–19; as medium of spiritual transcendence, 12–13, 19–36, 98; Christian epic and "double" mind portrayed by paradox of, 13, 118–20; as language of mind, 118–20; major and minor patterns summarized, 125; evolution of, 13, 125–131; decline of, 130–35; substitution of infinite diversity for, 133; division into discord and concord, 133–34; *see also* Wit
Dissentaneous arguments, 5–6
Discovery, as poetic principle, *see* Wit
Disorderly order, aesthetic concept of, 9, 10
Distortion of tenses, *see* Tense shifts
Divine Poems, The (Donne), 55, 126; *see also* "A Hymne to Christ"
"Divinitie" (Herbert), 50
Donato, Eugenio, 137, 141
Donne, John, 4–5, 12, 14–36, 82, 87, 93, 97, 132; comparison of style with later metaphysical verse, 36, 37–39, 49–50, 53, 55–56, 71–73, 90–91, 97, 98, 125–27
Drury, Elizabeth (subject of Donne's *Anniversaries*), identity and symbolism of, 25–26, 142; as pattern of excellence to emulate, 34–36, 132
Dualism, *see* Monism
Durr, R. A., 60, 144, 145

E. K., 9, 10
Eliot, T. S., 99–100
Emblem books, *frontispiece,* ix, 95, 137
Empedocles, 6–7, 8, 129
Epistles (Horace), 7
Essence and accident (philosophical terms of Being), 25, 28, 33–34; *see also* Truth
Eternity, *see* Time and Eternity
"Extasie, The" (Donne), 16, 18

Fall of Man, The: response to, in Donne, 33; in Marvell, 73, 76–97; in Milton, 101, 103–24; loss restored, 103; mind and language reflected by, 119–20; paradoxical world of man mirrored by, 127; restoration through science, 130
Fall, The "fortunate": Milton on, 98–124, 127–28; time and eternity in relation to, 109, 128; coincidence of opposites in connection with, 109; *see also* Regeneration
Fancy, linked with judgment, 3; as lesser faculty, 134; *see also* Imagination
Far-fetched analogy, 4
Farquhar, George, 3
Ferry, Anne Davidson, 101
Finney, Gretchen, 139
First Anniversary, The (Donne), 12; *see also Anniversaries*
Fish, Stanley, 112
"Flea, The" (Donne), 15
"Flower, The" (Herbert), 22
Ford, P. Jeffrey, 144
"Forerunners, The" (Herbert), 50
Freeman, Kathleen, 138–39
Freud, Sigmund, 119
Friedman, Donald, 146
"Funerall Elegie, A" (Donne), 35

Games, false complexities of, in Herbert, 37, 41–42, 46; *see also* Primero
"Garden, The" (Marvell), 75, 79–86
Gardner, Helen, 141
Garner, Ross, 144
"General" vs. "particular," as aesthetic values, 134
Gerusalemme liberata (Tasso), *see* Lombardelli, Orazio
Georgics (Virgil), 83, 85
"Gods Saints are shining lights" (Vaughan), 64
Goldstein, Harvey, 140
"Good-morrow, The" (Donne), 19

161

Index

"Goodfriday, 1613. Riding Westward" (Donne), 36, 55
Good and evil, moral choice between, 111-12
Guss, Donald, 141
Gracián, Baltasar, 4, 137
Gwynn, Frederick L., 146

Hardison, O. B., 142
Harmony: of discords within world, 7; as number, 7-8; application to poetry of number, weight, and measure, 8-10; musical, 8-9, 28, 29-30, 138-39; of tensions, 11-13, 125-30
Harris, Victor, 137, 140, 143
Hawkins, Henry, 95
Haydn, Hiram, 137, 140
Heraclitus, 6, 11-12, 72, 107; bow of, 12, 125
Herbert, George, 5, 6, 37-54, 85, 126-27; comparison with Donne's style, 37, 38, 39, 49-50; poetry as transitional, 53-54
Hidden plainness, poetic theory of, 43-46
Hill, D. M., 148
Hobbes, Thomas, 5, 134, 138, 150
Hollander, John, 139
Holmes, Elizabeth, 144, 145
"H. Scriptures I, The" (Herbert), 40
"H. Scriptures II, The" (Herbert), 22, 38, 39, 40
Horace, 7, 8
Hoskins, John, 138
Howard, Henry, *see* Surrey, Henry Howard, *Earl of*
Hugo, Hermann, *frontispiece*, ix
Huizinga, Johan, 20, 138, 141
Huntley, Frank L., 138
Hutchinson, F. E., 46
"Hymne to Christ, at the Authors last going into Germany, A" (Donne), 22-23

"I Walkt the other day" (Vaughan), 65-66
Illusion: in Milton, 107-08, 111-12, 115-16; *see also* Appearance vs. reality
Imagination, 3, 131, 132
Imprese, 4, 137
"Incarnation, and Passion, The" (Vaughan), 64
Interchangeable Course, or Variety of Things, Of the (Le Roy), 8, 139, 140
Infinite diversity, 133, 150
Infinity, 130, 133; *see also* Time
Inner vs. outer, *see* Appearance vs. reality

Interpretation of Dreams, The (Freud), 119
Invention, false, in Herbert, 37, 41-42, 45
Invention, as poetic principle, 21, 41, 45; *see also* Wit
Itrat-Husain, 144, 145

John of the Cross, *St.*, 58, 144-45
Johnson, Dr. Samuel: equation of metaphysical wit with *discordia concors*, 4-5; on changing fashions of wit, 11, 135
Jonson, Ben, 25, 79, 132
"Jordan (I)" (Herbert), 42-44, 46, 51
"Jordan (II)" (Herbert), 45-46
"Joy of my life!" (Vaughan), 64
Judgment and fancy: as components of wit, 3; subsequent division into separate faculties, 134
Juliana (character in Marvell's poetry), 77-78, 80, 83, 87

Kermode, Frank, 83
Killigrew, Anne, Mrs (subject of Dryden's poem), 132
King, A. H., 83
Kuttner, Stephan, 139

Language: as mirror of mind, 4 (*see also* Mind); changing notion of, 131; *see also* Punning language
La Primaudaye, Pierre de, 27
Leavis, F. R., 99
Legouis, Pierre, 94, 147
Le Roy, Louis, 8, 139, 140
Lewalski, Barbara, 142
Lewis, C. S., 137, 138
"Life of Cowley, The," *see* Johnson, Dr. Samuel
Logic, The Art of (Milton), 5; *see also* Dissentaneous arguments
Lombardelli, Orazio, 10-11
Lord, George deF., 145-46
"Love I" (Herbert), 41, 45-46, 52
"Love (II)" (Herbert), 41, 53
"Love (III)" (Herbert), 52-53
"Loves Alchymie" (Donne), 15-16

McCaffrey, Isabel G., 103, 149
Magna Instauratio (Bacon), 131-32
Manilius, Marcus, 12, 140
Manley, Frank, 25, 141
Margoliouth, H. M., 145-46
Martz, Louis, 137, 141, 147; *see also* Meditation
Marvell, Andrew, 5, 71-97; comparison of poetic style, 71-73, 87, 97, 98, 127-28; chronology of the poems, 145-46

Index

Materialism, philosophical, 135
Maurus, Rabanus, 95
Mazzeo, J. A., 137, 141, 142; *see also* "Correspondence, Poetic of"
Meditation, formal: as poetic principle, 4; in relation to the soul (*see also Anniversaries*), 35-36; *see also* Manley, Frank and Martz, Louis
Metaphor: changing nature of, 20-21; as mediating term between extremes, 20-21; creation of Elizabeth Drury (*Anniversaries*) as mediating metaphor to unite opposites, 32, 34-35; role of, in Donne, 20-25, 31-32, 34-36; in Herbert, 37-40, 46, 49-50; unusual use of, in Vaughan, 55-56; parodic pattern created by, 67-69; metaphysical vs. contemporary use of, 133
Metaphysical wit, *see* Wit
Migne, J.-P., 148
Milton, John, 5, 9, 68, 84-85, 91, 93, 98-124, 128-29, 131-32, 133
Miltonic similes: 98-124, 128-29; debate over their relevance, 99-102; a unity of opposites, 117; paradoxical nature of, 117, 118-20; imaginative time of, 117; reflection of mental activity, 118-20; *discordia concors* as narrative motif of *Paradise Lost*, 119-20; Satan-Ophiucus simile, 99-100; Satan-leviathan, 100; Satan-Moses, 102; universe-tree, 109-11; Satan-Christ in the "Sun-bright Chariot" (test simile), 104-108, 112, 113, 115-18, 122-24, 128; Satan in cloud and in eclipse, 114-15; Satan-Michael, 116-17; reflection of *discordia concors* as yoking of opposites in, 98-120; mirror of *discordia concors* as unity in multiplicity, 98, 120-124; mimetic imitation of epic theme and structure, 120
Mind: as wit, 3-4; effort to restore man's "double" mind to harmony, in Marvell, 78-80; garden of (*hortis mentis*), 80-81; reflection of postlapsarian life, 119; *discordia concors* the language of, 119-20; mirror of language and of universe, 131; opposing views on, 131-32; *see also* Wit
Miner, Earl, 138
Monism, in equipoise with dualism, 109-12
Mont Blanc, 135
Morning Orisons (Milton), as example of Christianized pattern of unity in multiplicity, 121-24
"Morning-watch, The" (Vaughan), 64-65
Moses, song of, in *Anniversaries*, 27-28

Mount of Olives: or, Solitary Devotions (Vaughan), 70
"Mount of Olives" (II) (Vaughan), 68
Mower (character in Marvell's poetry), 72, 76-78, 80
"Mower against Gardens, The" (Marvell), 78-79, 80, 92-93
"Mower to the Glo-Worms, The" (Marvell), 77
"Mower's Song, The" (Marvell), 76
Multiplicity, unity in, *see* Unity in multiplicity

Narrator, in *Paradise Lost*, 101, 123, 133
Nature: in Marvell, 76-82, 88, 91-93, 94, 96, 97; in Milton, 114-15, 121-22, 123-24; changing views of, 125, 131, 132, 134-35; *see also* Book of Nature
Nelson, Lowry, Jr., 147
New Atlantis (Bacon), 130
Newton, John, 11
Nicolson, Marjorie Hope, 25, 137, 142
"Night, The" (Vaughan), 57-59, 61, 68-70, 144, 145
Number, weight, and measure: cosmic principle of, 7-8; application to poetics, 8-10, 123

"Ode to Mrs Anne Killigrew" (Dryden), 132
Ogden, H. V. S., 139
"On a Drop of Dew" (Marvell), 84, 87-97, 98, 128
"On the Morning of Christ's Nativity" (Milton), 85, 114
Ong, Walter J., S. J., 138
Opposites: yoking of, 5-6, 12-13, 14-26, 119-20; coincidence of, 117; tension between, 125; *see also* Metaphor
Orator extemporaneus (Radau), 11
Ornstein, Robert, 142
Ovid, 7, 139
Oxymoron, 4

Paradise: restoration within mind, 85, 97, 103; recovery through science, 130; *see also* "On a Drop of Dew"
Paradise Lost (Milton), 9, 68, 81, 84-85, 91, 93, 98-124, 128-29; genre of, 102-03; epic themes of, 120, 128; as Christian epic, 118-19; dramatic vs. epic structure of, 123-24; comparison of first and second editions of, 123; circular structure of, 128; *see also* Miltonic similes
Paradise Regained (Milton), 94, 106
Parthenia sacra (Hawkins), 95

163

Index

Paradox: *discordia concors* associated with, 4, 126; Christian variety of, 13, 88; regeneration created by, in Vaughan, 55–70; as Miltonic philosophy, 111–12; engendered by the Fall, 127–28
Patterson, James, 148
Paul, *St.*, 44; *see also* Hidden plainness
Peter, John, 149
Petrarchan motifs, 41, 42, 52, 78, 83; "Jordan" poems (Herbert) as rejection of, 143; *see also* Juliana
Pettet, E. C., 56, 144, 145
Pia desideria (Hugo), *frontispiece; see also* Emblem books
Pico della Mirandola, Giovanni, 139
"Picture of Little T. C. in a Prospect of Flowers, The" (Marvell), 79
Phaeton myth, 75, 83, 146
Piepho, Edward Lee, 138
Plato, *see Timaeus*
Poetic creation, changing attitude toward nature of, 11–13, 130–31
Poetic theory of hidden plainness, in Herbert, 43–46; *see also* Primero
Poetics, 3–13, 132–35; *see also discordia concors*
Poetry: as "invention," 21, 41, 45; as "fiction" vs. "truth," 42; contribution of metaphysical poets to devotional, 13, 125–26; changing views of, 132
Pope, Alexander, 5, 129–30
Praz, Mario, 137
"Praise of the Dead, To the" (Donne), 28
Primero, 46–47, 51; *see also* Weller, Samuel
Progress, in time, 130
Prolepsis, 99–100; *see also* Miltonic similes
"Pulley, The" (Herbert), 47–48
Pun: paradoxical, 108; disparagement of (Addison), 134; *see also* Miltonic similes
Punning language: paradoxical quality of, 109–11; simultaneous assertion of monism and dualism, 109–11; expression of philosophical attitude by, 111–12
Pythagorean tetrad, 9; Christianized version, 122
Pythagoras, 7, 138; Aristotle on, 138; *see also* Number, weight, and measure

Radau, Michael, 11, 140
Rationalism, 135
Realism, scholastic, 20, 141; *see also* Baker, Herschel

Reality: older view as essence, 20–22; modern perception as flux, 132–33
Regeneration, poetic creation of, in Vaughan, 55–70; *see also* Paradise
"Regeneration" (Vaughan), 59–60, 61, 64, 69
Religio Medici, see Browne, Sir Thomas
"Religion" (Vaughan), 60–61, 62
Richome, Lewis, 95–96
Rickey, Mary Ellen, 144
Ricks, Christopher, 102, 149
Ryken, Leland, 147

Sandbank, S., 144
Sasek, Lawrence, 146
Satan (character in *Paradise Lost*), *see* Miltonic similes
Saveson, J. E., 148
Scholastic realism, *see* Realism
Scripture: role of, in Donne, 20–24; use of, in Herbert, 22, 37–54, 126–27; metaphorical interpretation of, 95; *see also* Metaphor
"Search, The" (Herbert), 6
Second Anniversary, The (Donne), 39, 72, 87, 91, 132; *see also* Anniversaries
Seneca, Lucius Annaeus, 7, 139
Sensibility, as aesthetic principle, 135
Sermons (Donne), 93, 140, 148; typical structure of, 90–91
"Shepheardes Calender, The" (Spenser), 10; a reflection of *discordia concors* as unity in multiplicity, 9
Sicherman, Carol Marks, 142
"Silence, and stealth of dayes!" (Vaughan), 60, 62, 67
Silex Scintillans (Vaughan), characterization of, 127; *see also* Vaughan, Henry
Similes, *see* Miltonic similes
Simmonds, James D., 144, 145
Singer, Samuel Weller, 144
"Sinner, The" (Herbert), 37–40
Skepticism, scientific, 135
Smith, A. J., 141
Solecism, poetic function of, 89–90; *see also* Tense shifts
Songs and Sonnets, The (Donne), 14–19; characterization of, 14, 19, 25, 72, 126
Soul: harmony of discords within human and world soul, 7–8; poetic "tuning" of, 10; activities of (*Anniversaries*), 35, 142; in Marvell, 71–97
Spenser, Edmund, 9, 10
Spitzer, Leo, 139, 140
Stanwood, P. G., 142, 143
"Starre, The" (Herbert), 85
Steadman, John, 149
Stevens, Wallace, 97

Index

Stewart, Stanley, 146
Strain, varieties in metaphysical verse, 24–25
Structure: *discordia concors* as circle of year, 7; universal discord harmonized by God, 8; circular shape a revelation of implicit harmony in *The Temple*, 52–53; in Marvell, eternity mirrored by circle, 79–80, 83; creation of circle by Christian annihilation, 88; soul reflected by circle, 91–94, 96–97; in Milton, epic theme and structure circular, 120–24, 128; five-act dramatic vs. epic, 123–24; poem as cosmic form without reference to publicly shared symbols, 131; *see also* Style
Style: as reflection of meaning, 3–13, 125–35; tension of human emotion a characteristic of, in Donne, 14–19, 126; role of metaphor in, 20–25; spiritual transcendence achieved by violent yoking, in Donne, 25–36; transition to greater allusiveness, in Herbert, 37–54; distinguished by paradoxical substructure, in Vaughan, 55–70; shift from yoking of opposites to unity in multiplicity, in Marvell, 71–97; in Miltonic similes, 98–124; in Marvell and Milton, circular structure in relation to, 128–29; stream of consciousness technique appropriate to reality as flux, 133; *see also* Wit
Sublimity, as aesthetic value, 134–35
Summers, Joseph, 144
"Sunne Rising, The" (Donne), 19
"Superliminare" (Herbert), 52
"Sure, there's a tye of Bodyes!" (Vaughan), 56, 61–64, 68
Surrey, Henry Howard, Earl of, 88
"Symbolist attitude," in Middle Ages, 20; *see also* Huizinga, Johan

Tasso, Torquato, 10, 140
Taste, as aesthetic principle, 135
Tayler, Edward W., 80–81, 137, 146, 150
Temple, The (Herbert), 37–54; characterization of the series, 37, 126–27; *see also* Herbert, George
Tense shifts: in Marvell, 81, 86–87, 89–90; in Milton, 147
Tension: a characteristic of metaphysical poetry, 11–13, 125–127; typical of relationship between physical and spiritual love, in Donne, 14–19; analogous to bow of Heraclitus, 12, 25, 72, 125, 127
Tesauro, Emmanuele, 4, 137, 141

"Thou that know'st for whom I mourne" (Vaughan), 63
Timber; or, Discoveries (Jonson), 132
Timaeus (Plato), 7
Time: 13, death as solution to, in Marvell, 72–76, 85–88; as image of eternity, 83; fulfillment in, 97; spatial aspect of, 117; as progress, 130; as infinity, 130, 133; *see also* Time and Eternity
Time and Eternity: 82–89, 124, 128; figural view of, 97, 98, 128–29; circle as symbol of, in Marvell, 82–89; in Milton, 109; *discordia concors* as circle in which God harmonizes discords, 139–40; *see also* Tense shifts
"To all Angels and Saints" (Herbert), 39, 40
"To his Coy Mistress" (Marvell), 74–75, 76, 83, 87
Toliver, Harold, 71, 83, 146, 147
Transcendence, spiritual, 12–13, 20–25, 37, 55, 71–73, 98, 124; versus non-transcendence, 11–13, 125–30
Travesty, of God, 108
"True Hymne, A" (Herbert), 49
Truth: as "essential" in philosophical sense, 20–22; metaphor as true, 21–22, 24; poetry to be read as, in Herbert, 40, 43–46; division of, at man's Fall, 103–04; changing perceptions of, 131–32; absolute vs. subjective, 133
Tuve, Rosemond, 143, 144

"Undertaking, The" (Donne), 17–18
Underwood, Horace H., 144
Unity in Multiplicity: as pattern of *discordia concors*, 5–6, 7–11, 13, 71, 97, 98, 121–24, 125, 128–29; *see also* "On a Drop of Dew"
Ut pictura poesis, Horatian principle of, 9

Vaughan, Henry, 4, 5; similarities to Herbert, 53–54; relationship to Donnean wit, 55–56; creation of paradoxes that represent regeneration, 55–70; position in evolution of metaphysical wit, 127; debate on role of nature in, 66–70, 145; as forerunner of romantic poets, 145
Virgil, 83, 85, 103
Vives, Juan Luis, 139

Waldock, A. J. A., 103
Wasserman, Earl, 5, 129, 132, 137, 138, 149–50
War in heaven (episode in *Paradise Lost*), 104–08, 112–18; *see also* Miltonic similes

Index

"Water-fall, The" (Vaughan), 66–67
Weinberg, Bernard, 140
Wellek, René, 137
Whaler, James, 99–100, 101, 102, 112
Wheelwright, Philip, 146
Widmer, Kingsley, 101–02
Williams, William Carlos, 133
Williamson, George, 138, 142
"Windsor Forest" (Pope), 5, 129–30
Wisdom, Book of, 7–8; *see also* Number, weight and measure
Wit: as mind, embracing both judgment and fancy, 3–4; modern connotation as cleverness or comic art, 3–4; equation of *discordia concors* with, 4–5, 11, 138, 140; definitions of, 4–5, 11; alternate theories of metaphysical wit, 4, 137; as "discovery" (or "invention") versus wit as "creation," 3, 21–22, 141; evolution of, 126–30, 137; God's inspiration of, 41–42, 52–53, 131; varieties of metaphysical wit summarized, 125–29; detrimental to understanding of world, 131–32; division into fancy and judgment, discord and concord, 3, 134, 137; changing concept of, 3–4, 135, 137; disparagement of, 150
"Wit, Of" (Cowley), 10
"Womans Constancy" (Donne), 14
Wonderful Woorkmanship of the World, The (Daneau), 9–10
World: as tenuous harmony of discords, 6–8, 11–12, 13; transcendence of, by violent yoking of opposites, 12–13, 25–36; as deceptive, in Vaughan, 66–70; symbolic potential diminished, 129; *see also* Nature

Yoking of opposites: 5–6, 11–13, 125; in Donne, 14–36; Herbert's use of, compared to Donne's, 37; in Herbert, 37–54; in Vaughan, 55–70; shift in Marvell from yoking of opposites to unity in multiplicity, 71, 87–88; in Milton, 98–121; *see also* Miltonic similes